CROCHETED
Lampshades

CROCHETED
Lampshades

DILYS A. FRONKS

Dryad Press Ltd
London

A C K N O W L E D G M E N T

My thanks to Roger the photographer and motivator, and to Tamana and Tessa my companions in relaxation

Photography by Roger C. Fronks

First published 1987

ISBN 0 8521 9674 1

Typeset by Servis Filmsetting Ltd, Manchester
and printed in Great Britain by
The Bath Press Ltd
Bath, Avon
for the publishers
Dryad Press Ltd
8 Cavendish Square
London W1M 0AJ

Contents

Introduction

The inspiration for this book came to me whilst watching a friend labouring over a macramé lampshade. 'Surely you can find an easier way of doing this in crochet' she muttered. After extensive experimenting with wools, strings and cords, I eventually stumbled on dishcloth/handicraft cotton. This provided a washable and soft-textured fabric which gave the right amount of stretch to the covers. Using two balls together provided a better thickness, thus eliminating the need to line the shades. I tended to prefer the natural colour, but it is also perfect for dyeing. This book contains 12 patterns for a variety of shades and instructions for all the stitches mentioned. There is also advice on how to adapt the patterns to frames of other sizes.

I hope the book provides pleasure in achievement and inspires you to experiment further with different yarns and other size hooks.

D.A.F.

ONE

CROCHET: *The basic techniques*

To crochet is to make a succession of loops, using yarn and a hook, working with one loop on the hook at a time. More loops may be added during the execution of a stitch, but one loop is left on the hook after each stitch is completed.

HOLDING THE HOOK

(Left-handed workers should reverse the instructions, reading left for right and right for left.)

Right hand
The right hand holds and works the hook. Hold the hook like a pencil, at the flattened part, between the thumb and first finger. Let it rest against the second finger, with the tip of the hook pointing towards the thumb (fig. 1).

Left hand
The left hand holds the work and controls the supply of yarn from the ball towards the hook. Pinch the yarn between the thumb and first finger. Then place the yarn over the first and second fingers and under the third. Winding the yarn round the little finger helps to control the flow (fig. 2). By opening the first and second fingers, a space is created in which the hook will work the yarn (fig. 3). The middle finger will pull gently against the loop on the hook to ease the supply of yarn through the fingers. The thumb and finger should always be directly underneath each stitch being made.

THE STITCHES

All the instructions that follow are illustrated for simplicity using one ball of yarn, although the patterns that are included in this book use two balls of yarn together. Use a 5.00mm crochet hook for practising the basic stitches and when you can do these well, follow the same instructions but with two balls of

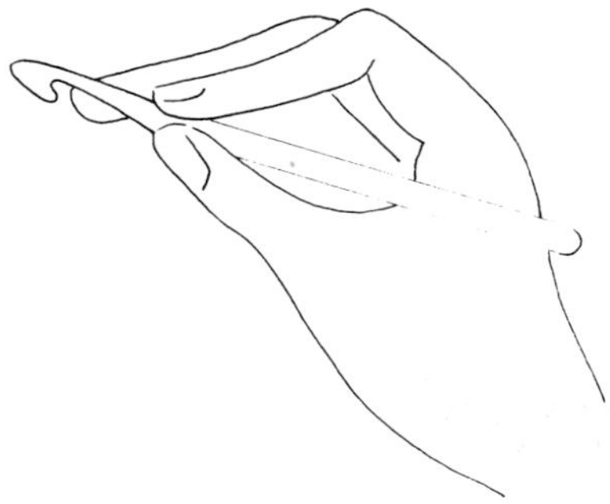

Fig. 1

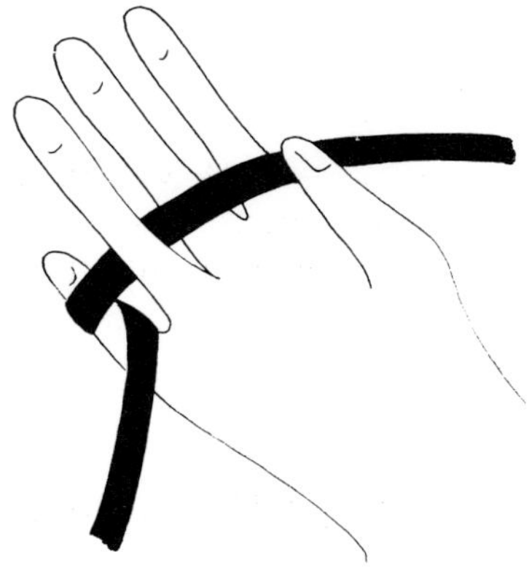

Fig. 2

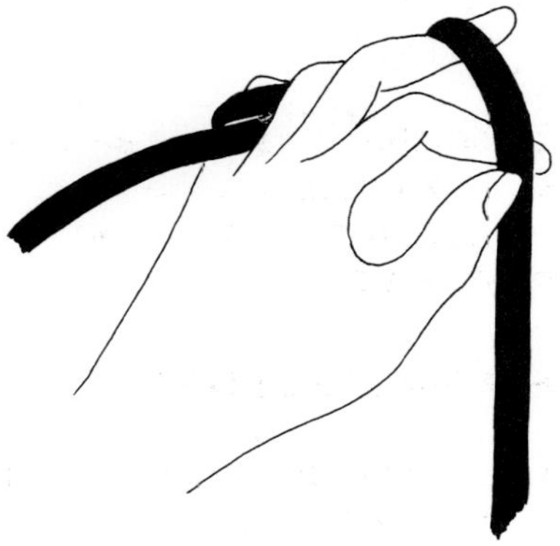

Fig. 3

yarn together. This may require some practice until you feel confident enough to prepare the tension square for comparison (see page 18).

THE SLIP LOOP

To produce the first working loop on the hook, make a slip loop (figs 4 and 5).

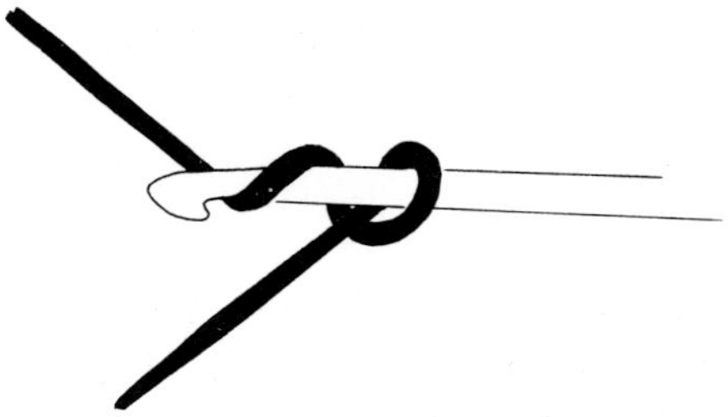

Fig. 4

Fig. 5

THE CHAIN (ch)

The chain is the starting stitch for all crochet projects and the number required will vary from the few needed to form a ring to start a square or circular motif, to the many needed to make up the base row for a larger piece of work.

To work a chain stitch
With the yarn held by the left hand and a slip loop on the hook in the right hand (fig. 6), wind the yarn round the hook by taking the hook over the yarn into the working space and under the yarn again (figs 7 and 8). Draw the yarn through the loop on the hook. One chain has been made, leaving one loop on the hook again. Repeat this for the number of chains required, not counting the slip loop or the chain left on the hook (fig. 9).
Rhythm: it may help you to repeat to yourself, 'yarn round hook, pull through chain' as you practise each stitch.

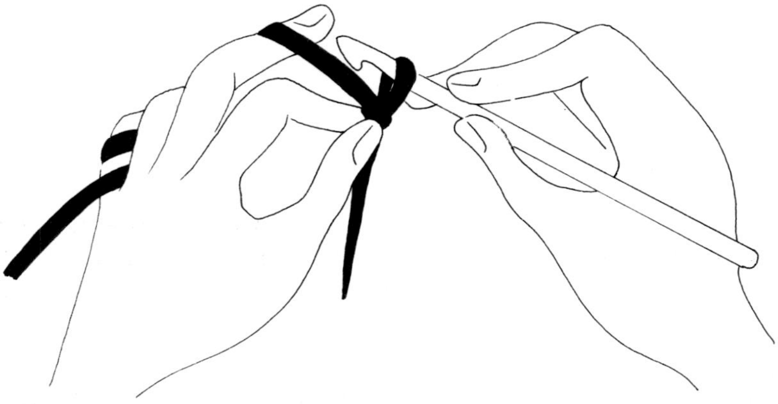

Fig. 6

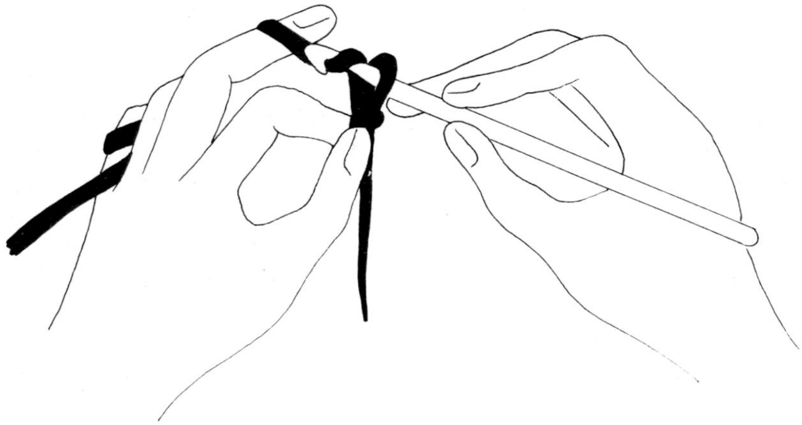

Fig. 7

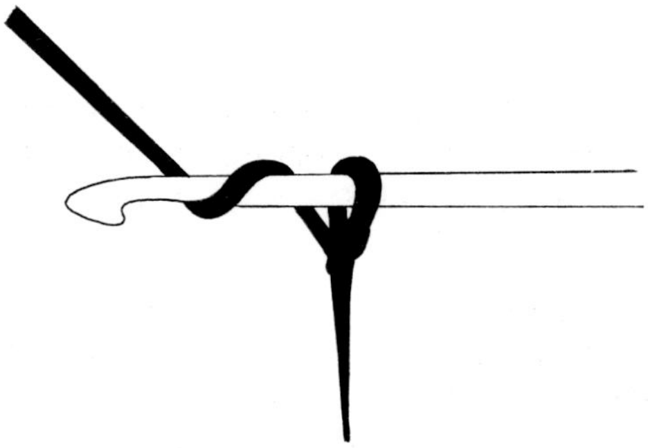

Fig. 8

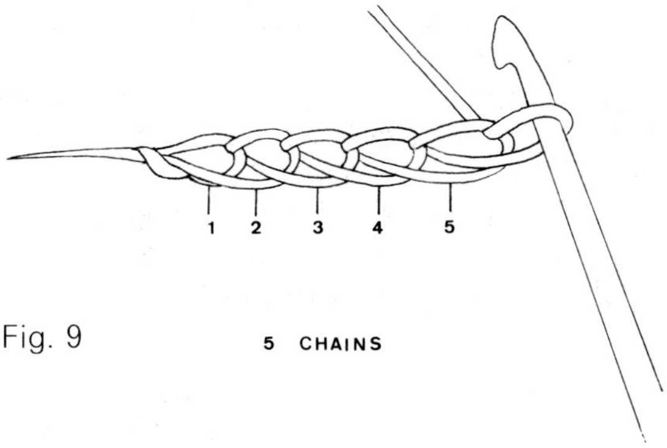

Fig. 9

5 CHAINS

THE DOUBLE CROCHET (dc)

For a practice piece make 11 chains. In order to work back along this row of chains it is necessary to 'step up' onto the next level. For a double crochet we use two chains for this purpose and these two chains will be said to stand for the first double crochet.

Inserting the hook
Looking at a row of chains it can be seen that there are three threads to each chain stitch (see fig. 9). When making other stitches back along this row it is necessary to insert the hook from the front to the back through the chains. On the base row I do this so that there is one thread above the hook and two threads below.

To work a double crochet
After making sure that the row of chains is not twisted, insert the hook from front to back into the third chain from the hook (fig. 10). Wind the yarn round the hook (fig. 11) and draw it back through the loop of the chain stitch (fig. 12). There are now two loops on the hook. Wind the yarn round the hook again (fig. 13) and draw it through both loops on the hook. A double crochet has been completed (fig. 14) and one loop is left on the hook. Repeat this process into each chain stitch.

If you need to do a double crochet on the top of another stitch on any row other than the base row, put the hook through the *two* loops at the top of the stitch.

Rhythm: it may help you to repeat to yourself, 'hook through loop, yarn round hook, pull back through loop, yarn round hook, pull through both'.

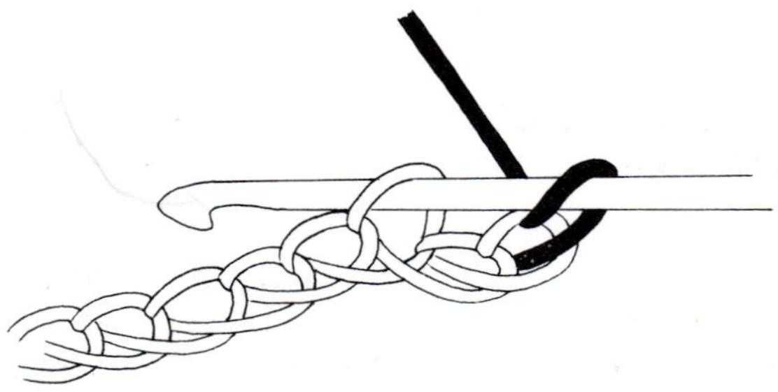

Fig. 10

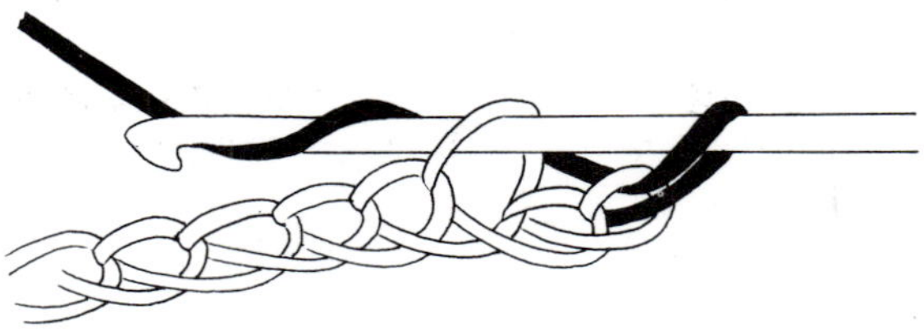

Fig. 11

Fig. 12

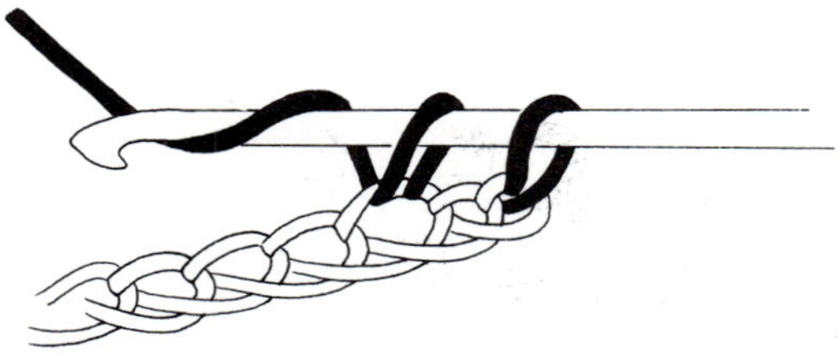

Fig. 13

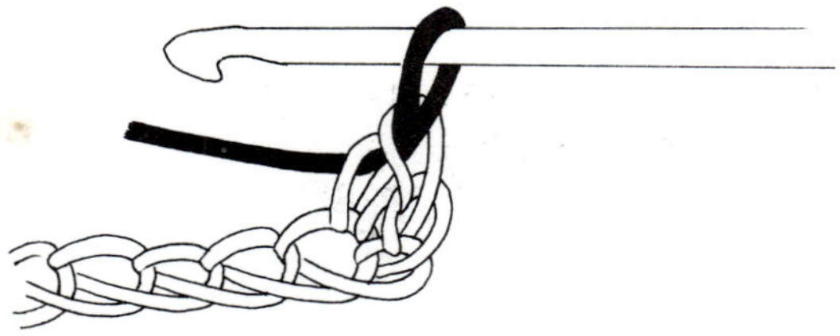

Fig. 14

THE TREBLE (tr)

For a practice piece make 12 chains. Working back along this row three chains will act as the 'step up' onto the next level, and will also stand for the first treble.

To work a treble
Wind the yarn round the hook and insert the hook from front to back into the fourth chain from the hook. Wind the yarn round the hook again (fig. 15) and draw the yarn back through the chain loop, leaving three loops on the hook (fig. 16). Wind the yarn round the hook again (fig. 17) and draw the yarn through two loops (fig. 18), wind the yarn round the hook again and draw through the remaining two loops. This leaves one loop on the hook and one treble has been completed (fig. 19).

Repeat this process into each of the practice chains to the end of the row (ten trebles). Turn back along the row making three chains for the 'step up' and to act as the first treble.

Continue making trebles going into the two loops at the top of each stitch each time.

Rhythm: it may help you to repeat to yourself, 'yarn round hook, hook through loop, yarn round hook, pull back through loop. Yarn round hook, pull through two; yarn round hook, pull through two'.

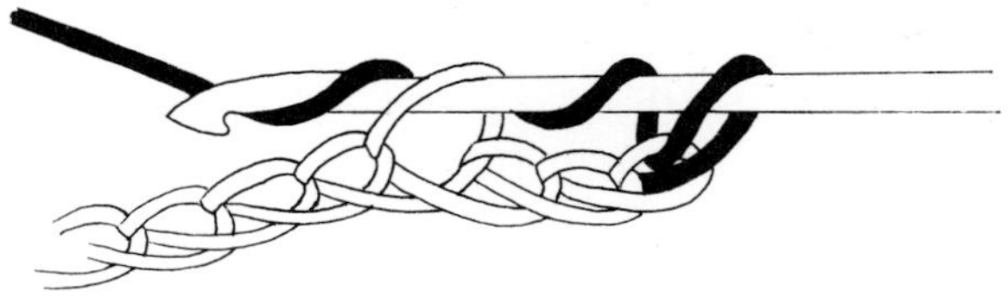

Fig. 15

Fig. 16

Fig. 17

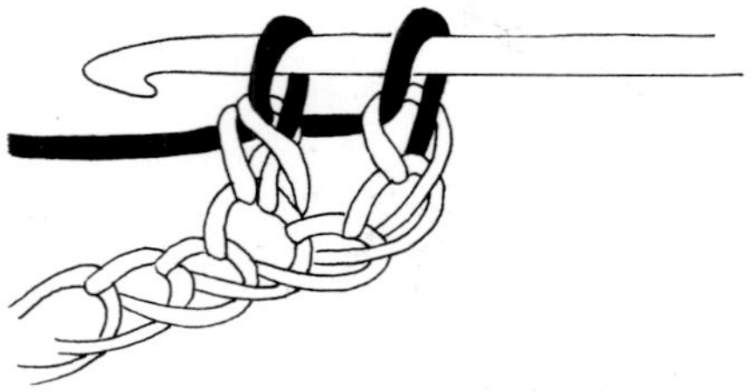

Fig. 18

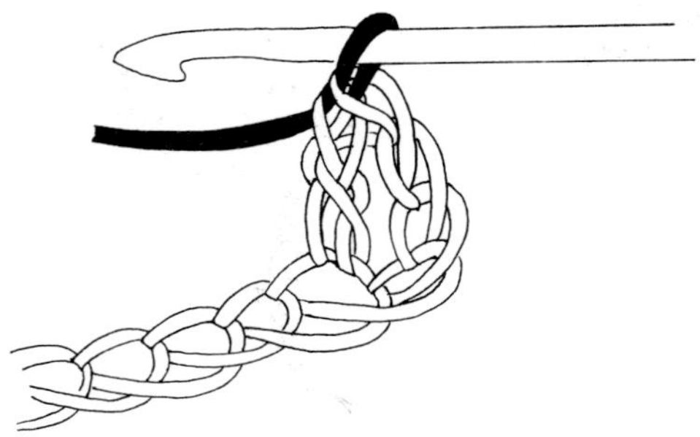

Fig. 19

THE HALF TREBLE (htr)

For a practice piece make 11 chains. Working back along this row of chains, two chains will act as the 'step up' to the next level and will also stand for the first half treble.

To work a half treble
Wind the yarn round the hook and insert it from front to back into the third chain from the hook (fig. 20).

Wind the yarn round the hook again and draw this back through the chain loop, leaving three loops on the hook (fig. 21).

Wind the yarn round the hook again (fig. 22) and draw the yarn through all three loops on the hook. This leaves one loop on the hook and one half treble has been completed (fig. 23).

Repeat the process into each of the following chains to the end of the row (ten half trebles). Turn back along the line using two chains to 'step up' and stand for the first half treble, and continue making half trebles, going into the two loops at the top of each stitch of the row below.
Rhythm: it may help you to repeat to yourself, 'yarn round hook, hook through loop, yarn round hook, pull back through loop. Yarn round hook, pull through all three'.

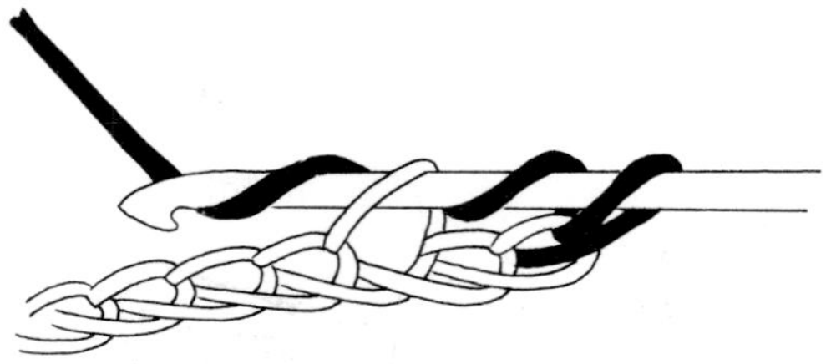

Fig. 20

Fig. 21

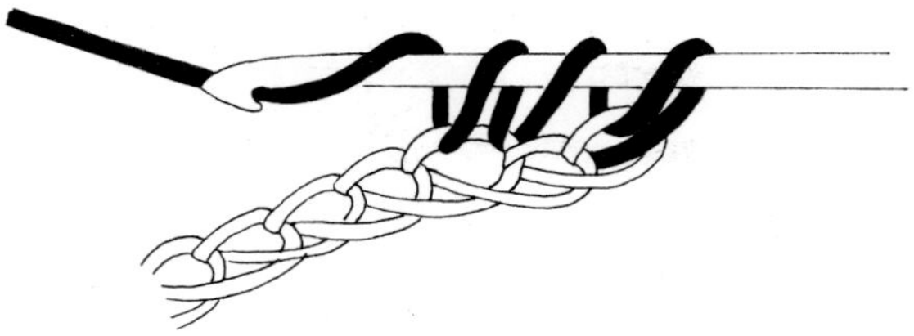

Fig. 22

Fig. 23

THE DOUBLE TREBLE (dtr)

Make 13 chains for a practice piece. Working back along this row of chains, four chains will act as the 'step up' to the next row and will also stand for the first double treble.

To work a double treble
Wind the yarn round the hook twice and insert the hook from front to back into the fifth chain from the hook (fig. 24).

Wind the yarn round the hook (fig. 25) and draw it back through the chain loop, leaving four loops on the hook (fig. 26).

Wind the yarn round the hook and draw it through two loops, leaving three loops on the hook (fig. 27). Repeat this step again to leave two loops on the hook (fig. 28), and again to leave one loop on the hook and to complete the double treble (fig. 29).

Repeat this process into each of the practice chains to the end of the row (ten double trebles). Turn back along the line using four chains to 'step up' onto the next level and to stand for the first double treble. Continue along this row going under the two loops at the top of the stitch each time.
Rhythm: it may help you to repeat to yourself, 'yarn round hook, yarn round hook, hook through loop, yarn round hook pull back through loop. Yarn round hook, pull through two, yarn round hook, pull through two, yarn round hook pull through two'.

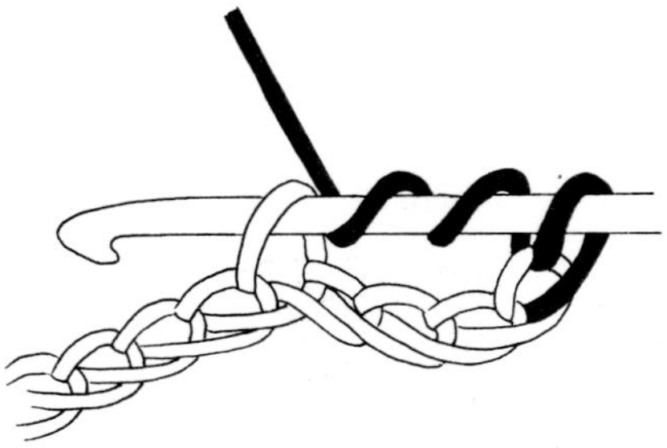

Fig. 24

Fig. 25

Fig. 26

Fig. 27

Fig. 28

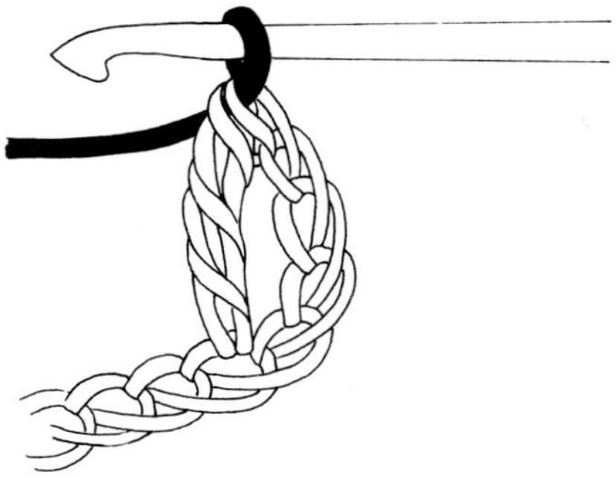

Fig. 29

THE SLIP STITCH (ss)

This is generally used to join the end of a row to the beginning in a circle, or for moving the hook invisibly along the work, without having to break off the yarn.

To work a slip stitch
For a practice piece make a number of chains. To join them into a ring, insert the hook from the front to the back of the first chain made. Make sure that the line of chains is not twisted and that the hook goes into the chain so that there are two loops above and one loop below. Wind the yarn round the hook (fig. 30) and draw it straight through the chain loops and the loop on the hook in one movement (fig. 31). A slip stitch has been completed and there is one loop on the hook.

If you are asked to slip stitch into a space, insert the hook into the space and draw the yarn through the space and the loop on the hook all in one movement. To slip stitch along other stitches, insert the hook under the two loops at the top of each stitch and draw the yarn through the stitch and the loop in one movement.

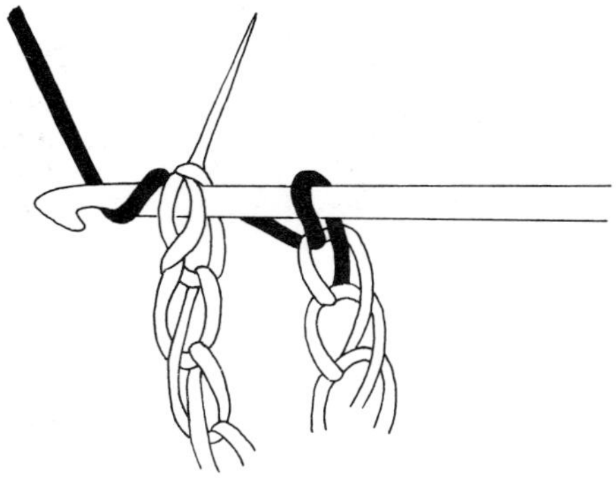

Fig. 30

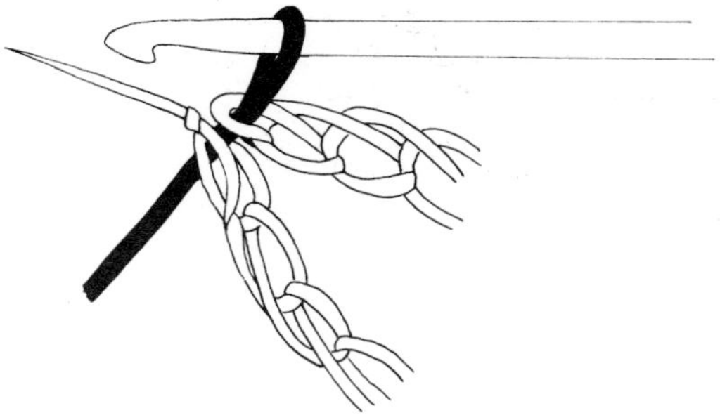

Fig. 31

FASTENING OFF

To fasten off permanently after completing the final stitch, cut the yarn about three inches from the work and pull the end through the loop left on the hook. Tighten gently.

After a slip stitch, a neater finish is given by the following method.

Complete the slip stitch according to the pattern, keeping the final loop on the hook. Cut the yarn about 7·5cm (3in) from the work and insert the hook into the next stitch. Wind the remaining yarn round the hook and draw the end through the stitch and the loop on the hook and tighten gently. The end can be woven into the work using a smaller hook or a darning needle.

JOINING IN NEW YARN

It is best to join in a new ball where the stitches are close together and when a stitch is in progress. When there are only 7·5 to 10cm (3 to 4in) of yarn left, continue making the stitch until the final stage is reached. This will usually mean that there are two loops left on the hook, except in the case of the half treble when there will be three loops. Lay the finishing yarn on top of the previous line, in the direction of work, and simply loop the new yarn over the hook (fig. 32). Pull this through to complete the stitch (fig. 33). Place the end of the new yarn on top of the end of the finishing yarn and continue with the pattern, working over the ends.

When using two balls together as in the patterns in this book, it will be necessary to stagger the joining in of the two new balls. It is worth noting here that the yarn will run more freely if you start with the end which is in the middle of the ball. This can usually be located and pulled out gently.

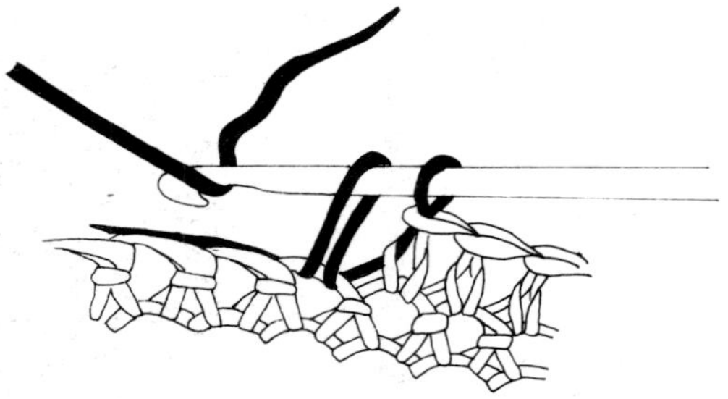

Fig. 32

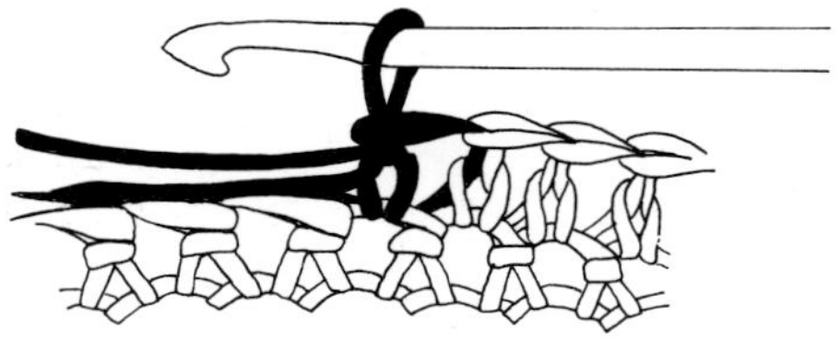

Fig. 33

THE RIGHT SIDE OF THE WORK

All my patterns are worked in a ring, in the same direction. Therefore the right side of the work will always be the side you are looking at while you work. This side will always go to the outside of the frame.

HOOK SIZES

I have used only one hook throughout this book and that is a 5.00mm hook, based on the International Standard Range (ISR).

ABBREVIATIONS

English		*American equivalent*	
ch	chain	ch	chain
dc	double crochet	sc	single crochet
htr	half treble	hdc	half double crochet
tr	treble	dc	double crochet
dtr	double treble	tr	treble crochet
st(s)	stitch(es)		
ss	slip stitch		
yrh	yarn round hook		

TENSION

It is important that you read this section before attempting any of the patterns that follow.

In crocheting terms, tension refers to the number of stitches and rows done over a given measurement. Quite naturally, it varies from person to person because it is dependent on how you hold your hook and how relaxed and rhythmical a worker you are. Obviously, fingers that are tense, produce work that is tight and difficult. I shudder to think how many times I have repeated my patterns over the years, but during the process, I have learnt to produce them at

Fig. 34

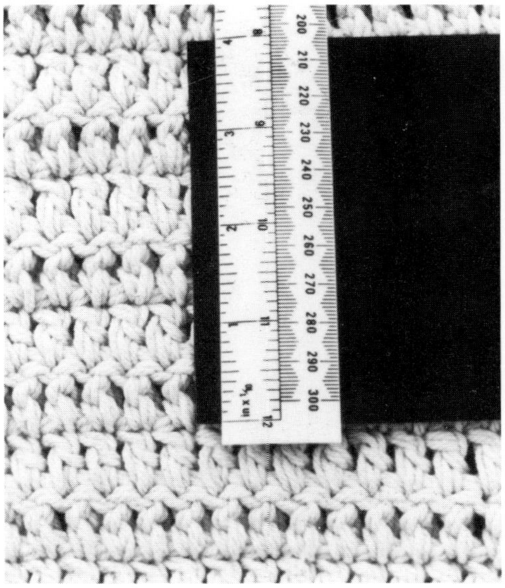

Fig. 35

speed efficiently and I have adjusted to the mechanics of using the yarn double. So, to cope with the bulk of the yarn and to allow for the finished cover to stretch over the frame, I have developed my own tension. For the patterns to work for you, it is necessary for you to closely match my tension sample.

For your comparison I have worked a sample piece in trebles using two balls of dishcloth/handicraft cotton and working on a 5.00mm hook. A block of 20 trebles over 6in should give you an adequately-sized piece for comparison.

Trebles worked on a 5.00mm hook give 10 stitches over 4in (fig. 34).

Trebles worked on a 5.00mm hook give 6 rows over 4in (fig. 35).

If you have *less* rows and stitches, your tension is *too loose* and you should change to a hook which is one size *smaller.* If you have *too many* rows and stitches, your tension is *too tight* and you should change to a hook which is one size *larger.*

Continue practising until a good match is made, changing hooks again if necessary.

TWO

The FRAMES

TYPES OF FRAMES

For the purposes of this book, it is preferable to use frames that are plastic coated, thus making the completed frame washable.
fig. 36 Bowed tulip
fig. 37 Cannister drum
fig. 38 Round drum
fig. 39 Bowed empire
fig. 40 Tiffany

Fig. 36

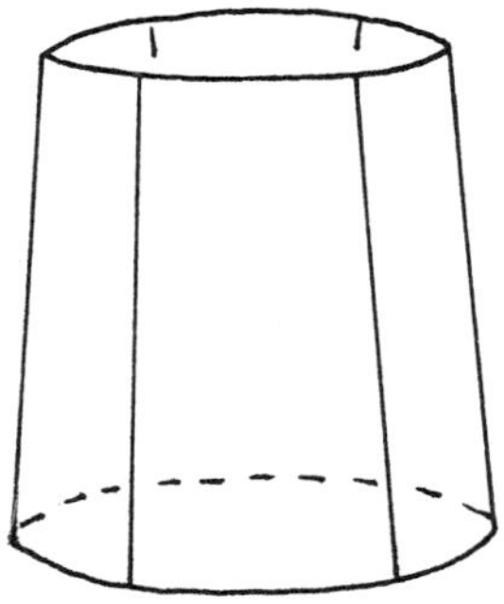

Fig. 37

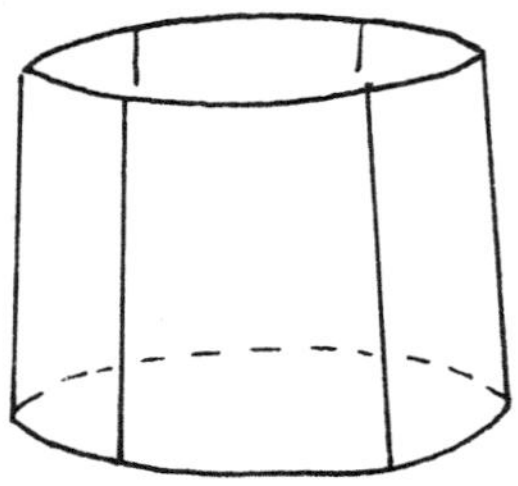

Fig. 38

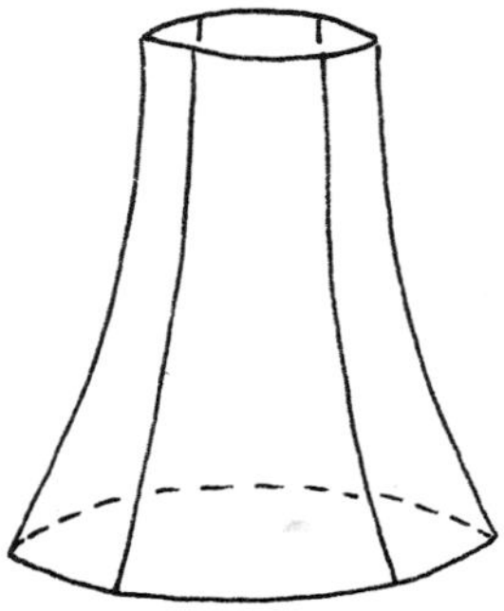

Fig. 39

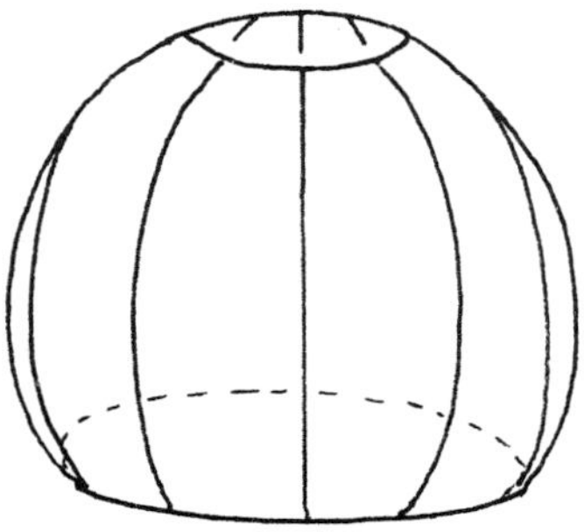

Fig. 40

BINDING THE FRAME

If you are unable to find a plastic-coated frame, or wish to re-cycle an old frame, binding will be necessary.

Binding tape can be purchased specially for the purpose and, to estimate the amount, measure the length of all the wire which makes up the frame and double it. (Bias binding may be used as an alternative, with one side ironed open.)

BINDING THE VERTICAL STRUTS

Start at the top of a vertical strut and, using binding tape which is one and a half times the length of the strut, loop the tape over the 'T' junction (fig. 41).

The first wrap round the strut will secure the end (fig. 42).

Wind the tape tightly, on the diagonal, down the strut as neatly as possible, just covering the edge of the tape above each time (fig. 43).

Finish off by wrapping the tape round the ring on both sides and pulling the end through in a knot (fig. 44). You can test that the binding is tight and secure by rolling the bound wire between the thumb and finger. The binding should not move at all.

Repeat the procedure for each vertical strut.

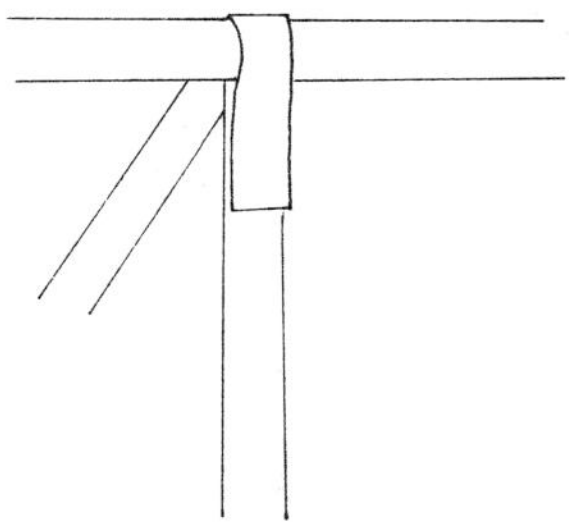

Fig. 41

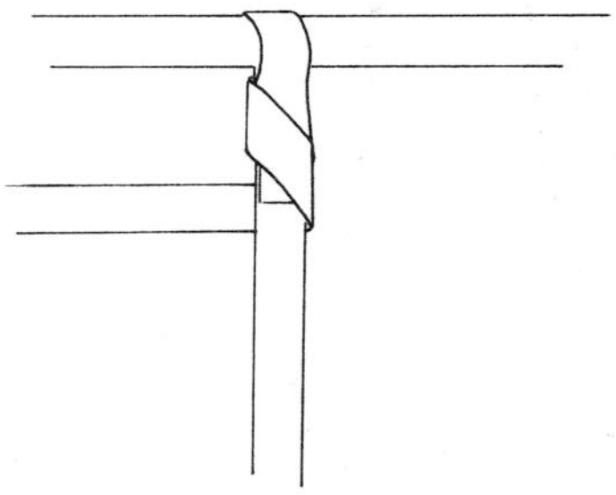

Fig. 42

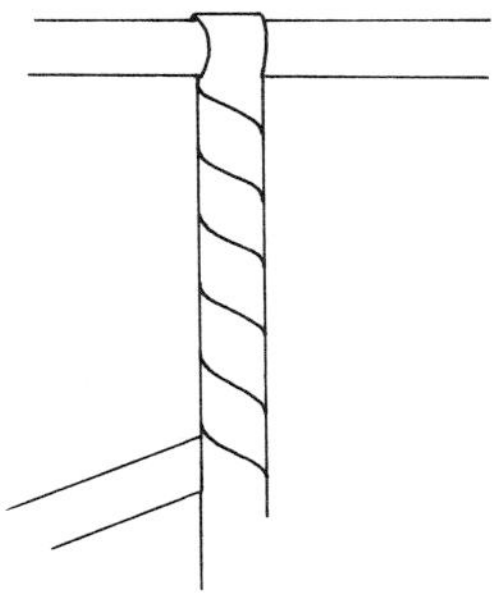

Fig. 43

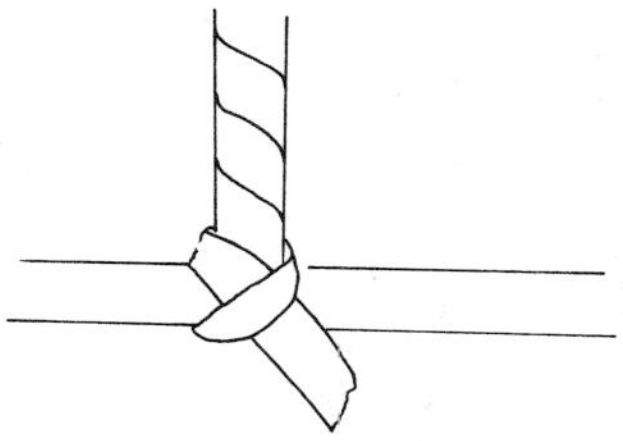

Fig. 44

BINDING THE RINGS

Cut binding tape which is twice the length of the ring.

Start at the top of the frame where a vertical strut meets the ring (fig. 45) and secure the end of the tape with the first turn (fig. 46).

Bind as tightly as possible, keeping an acute angle and just covering the edge of the previous turn.

When you come to the junction where a vertical strut meets the ring, make a figure-of-eight around the join (figs. 47 and 48).

Finish the ring with a knot to secure the end.

Repeat the procedure for the lower ring, trapping and covering all the ends left from binding the struts. Any remaining ends will be covered when the crochet is done round the rings.

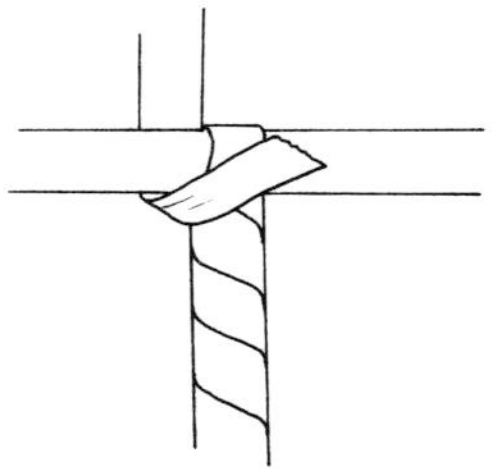

Fig. 45

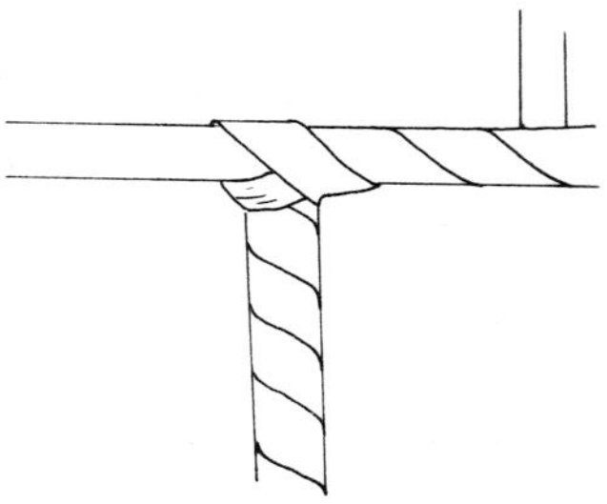

Fig. 46

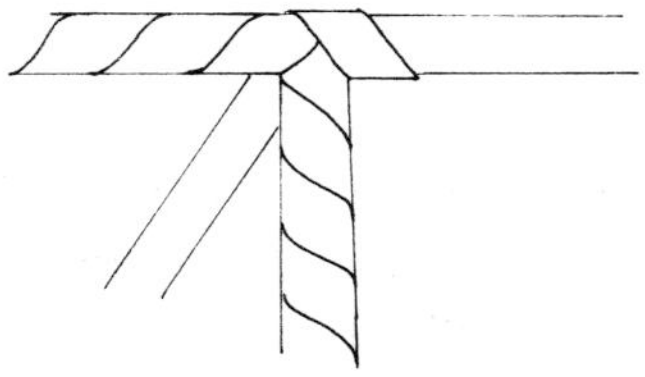

Fig. 47

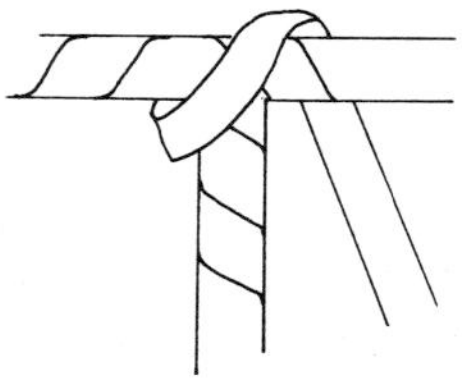

Fig. 48

THREE

The PATTERNS

CANNISTER DRUM 15cm (6in) (fig. 49)

Materials
Cannister drum frame (fig. 50)
2 × 100g balls of dishcloth/handicraft cotton
5.00mm hook

Stitches used

chain	ch
double crochet	dc
treble	tr
slip stitch	ss

Tension See page 18

Work using yarn double, pattern worked in multiples of four
Row 1 36 ch, ss into first ch to form ring. Check that this fits around top of frame (36 ch).
Row 2 1 dc into same st as ss, 1 dc into each st of ring, ss into first dc to form ring (36 dc).
Row 3 3 ch to stand for first tr, 1 tr into next 2 dc to make a block of 3 tr. Make 1 tr loosely into the dc before the first tr. *Miss 1 dc, 1 tr into each of next 3 sts. Make 1 tr loosely across tr block into the dc missed*. Repeat from * to * 7 times more. Ss into top of first tr to form a ring (9 tr blocks).
Row 4 1 dc into same st as ss, 1 dc into each st around the ring. Ss into first dc to form a ring (36 dc).
Rows 5–12 Rows 3 and 4 form the pattern. Repeat these rows four times more.

Fasten off and secure end. Close-up of pattern (fig. 51).

Measured length of unstretched cover 13·75cm ($5\frac{1}{2}$in).

Stretch cover over frame with Row 1 at the top and secure using 1 dc into each st around both rings (see page 47).

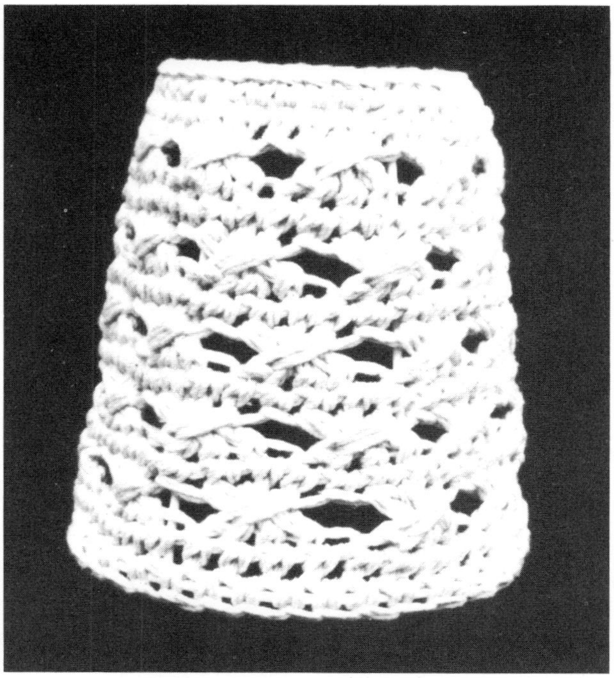

Fig. 49

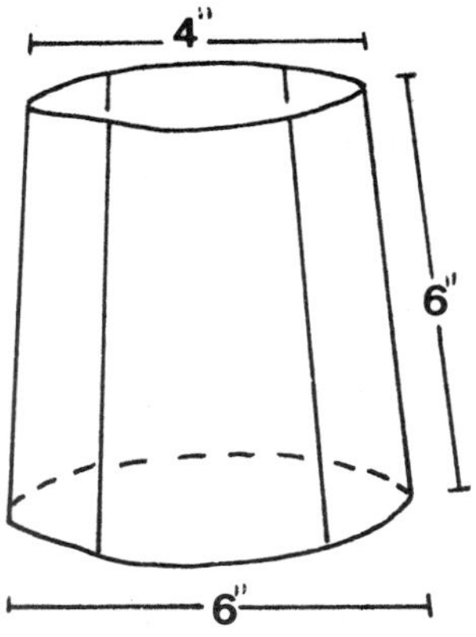

Fig. 50

Fig. 51

CANNISTER DRUM 20cm (8in) (fig. 52)

Materials

Cannister drum frame (fig. 53)
2 × 100g balls of dishcloth/handicraft cotton
5.00mm hook

Stitches used

chain	ch
double crochet	dc
treble	tr
slip stitch	ss

Tension See page 18

Work using yarn double, pattern worked in multiples of five

Row 1 60 ch, ss into top of first ch to form a ring. Check that this fits around top of frame (60 ch).

Row 2 1 dc into same st as ss. 1 dc into each st of ring, ss into first dc to form ring (60 dc).

Row 3 3 ch to stand for first tr, 4 more tr into same base st. *Miss 4 sts, 5 tr into next st*. Repeat from * to * 10 times more. Ss into top of first tr to form a ring (12 × 5 tr shells).

Fig. 52

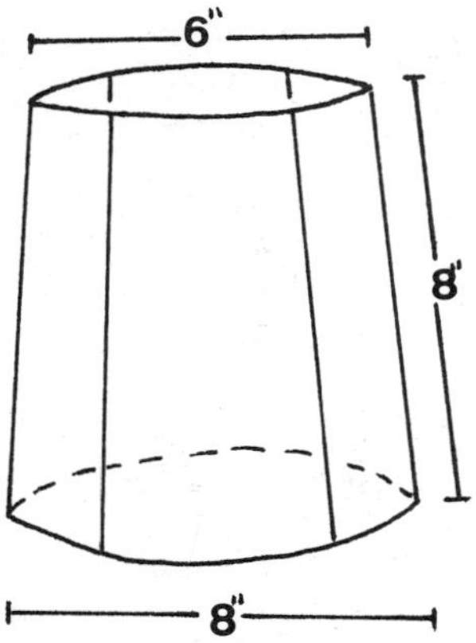

Fig. 53

Row 4 Ss along 2 sts to centre tr, 3 ch to stand for first tr, 4 tr into same base st. *Miss 4 sts, 5 tr into next st*. Repeat from * to * 10 times more. Ss into top of first tr to form ring.
Rows 5–9 Repeat *Row 4* 5 times more.
Row 10 Ss along 2 sts to centre tr, 1 dc into this st, 5 ch. *Miss 4 sts, 1 dc into next st, 5 ch*. Repeat from * to * 10 times more. Ss into first dc to form ring (12 ch loops).
Row 11 1 dc into same st as ss, 1 dc into each st around the ring. Ss into first dc to complete the ring (72 dc).

Fasten off and secure end. Close-up of pattern (fig. 54).

Measured length of unstretched cover 17·5cm (7in).

Stretch cover over frame, with Row 1 at the top, and secure using 1 dc into each st around both rings (see page 47).

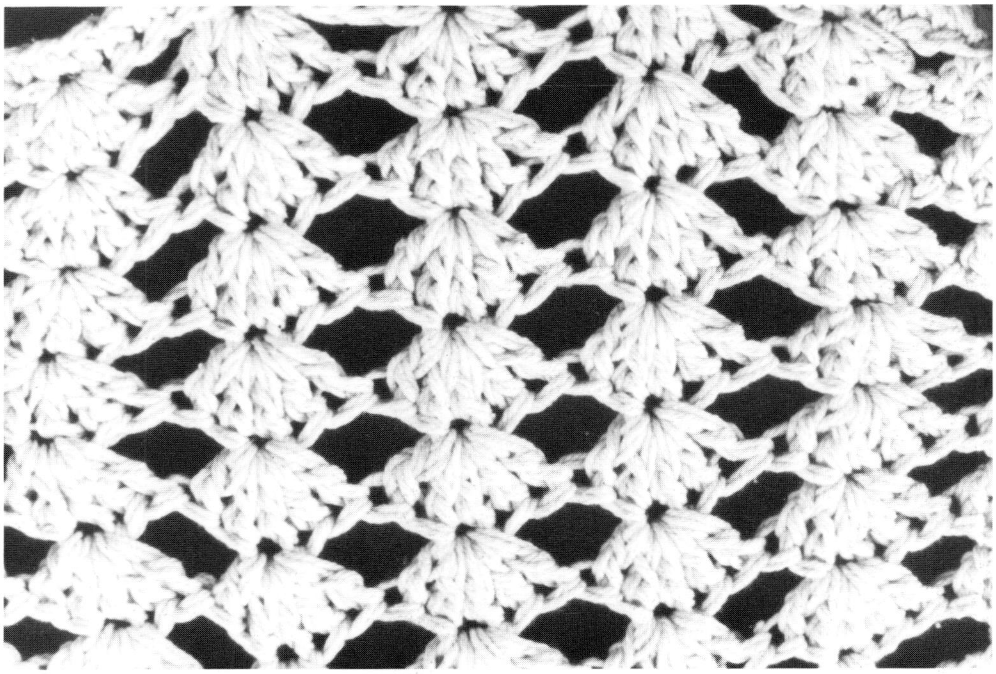

Fig. 54

CANNISTER DRUM 25cm (10in) (fig. 55)

Materials
Cannister drum frame (fig. 56)
2 × 100g balls dishcloth/handicraft cotton
5.00mm hook

Stitches used

chain	ch
double crochet	dc
half treble	htr
slip stitch	ss

Tension See page 18

Work using yarn double, pattern worked in multiples of eight
Row 1 72 ch, ss into first ch to form ring. Check that this fits around top of frame (72 ch).
Row 2 2 ch to stand for first htr, 1 htr into each st of ring. Ss into first htr to form ring (72 htr).
Row 3 1 dc into same st as ss, 1 dc into each of next 4 sts, 4 ch. *Miss 3 sts, 1 dc into next 5 sts, 4 ch*. Repeat from * to * 7 times more. Ss into first dc to form ring (9 pattern blocks).

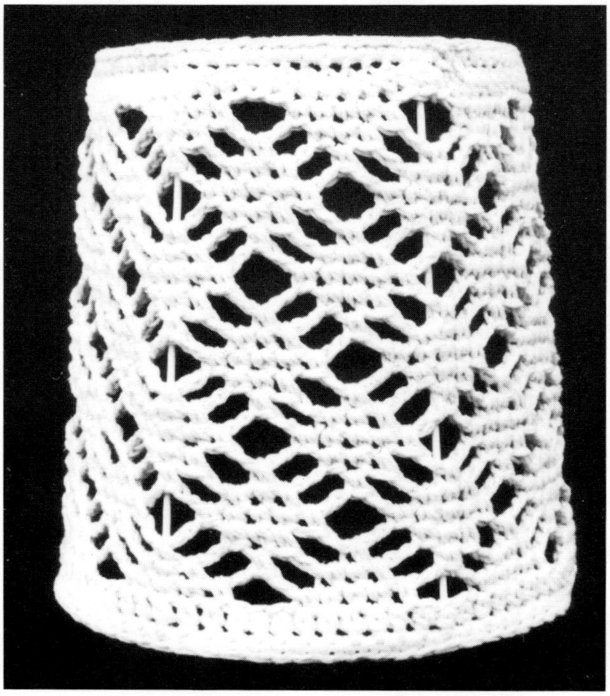

Fig. 55

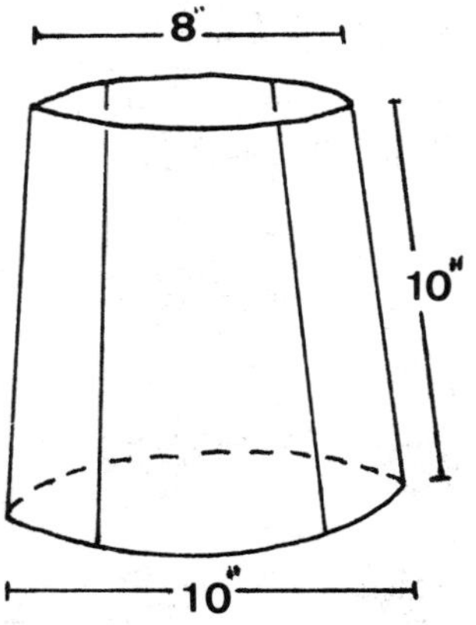

Fig. 56

Row 4 Ss into next dc, 1 dc into same st, 1 dc into next 2 sts, 3 ch, 1 dc into ch loop. *3 ch, miss 1 dc, 1 dc into next 3 sts, 3 ch, 1 dc onto ch loop*. Repeat from * to * 7 times more. 3 ch, ss into first dc to form ring.
Row 5 Ss into next dc, 1 dc into same st, 3 ch, 1 dc into ch loop, 1 dc into next dc, 1 dc into ch loop. *3 ch, 1 dc into centre dc, 3 ch, 1 dc into ch loop, 1 dc into next dc, 1 dc into ch loop*. Repeat from * to * 7 times more. 3 ch, ss into first dc to form ring.
Row 6 Ss along 2 ch of ch loop, 1 dc into same ch loop, 1 dc into each of next 3 dc, 1 dc into ch loop. *4 ch, 1 dc into next ch loop 1 dc into each of next 3 dc, 1 dc into ch loop*. Repeat from * to * 7 times more. 4 ch, ss into first dc to form ring.
Rows 7–21 Rows 4, 5 and 6 form the pattern. Repeat these rows 5 times more.
Row 22 2 ch to stand for first htr, 1 htr into each st around the ring. Ss into first htr to complete ring (81 htr).

Fasten off and secure end. Close up of pattern (fig. 57).

Measured length of unstretched cover 22·5cm (9in).

Stretch over the frame with Row 1 at the top and secure using 1 dc into each st around both rings (see page 47).

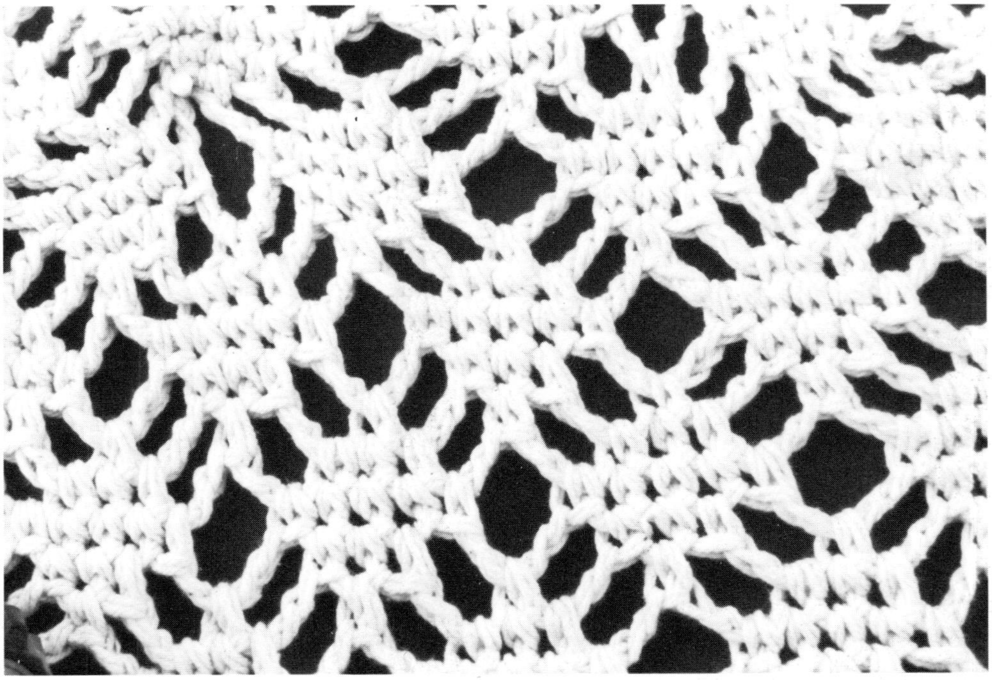

Fig. 57

CANNISTER DRUM 35cm (14in) (fig. 58)

Materials

Cannister drum frame (fig. 59)
6 × 100g balls dishcloth/handicraft cotton
5.00mm hook

Stitches used

chain	ch
slip stitch	ss
half treble	htr
double treble	dtr

Tension The width of each dtr shell is 3in (fig. 60). The length of the centre dtr in the shell is 2in (fig. 61). See page 18 for reference to tension.

Work using yarn double, pattern worked in multiples of eight

Row 1 96 ch, ss into first ch to form ring. Check that this fits around top of frame (96 ch).

Row 2 2 ch to stand for first htr, 1 htr into each st of ring. Ss into top of first htr to form ring (96 htr).

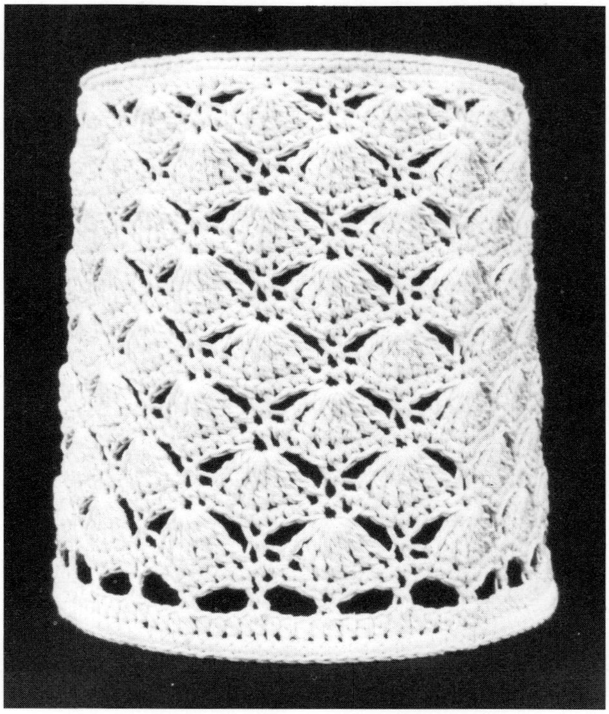

Fig. 58

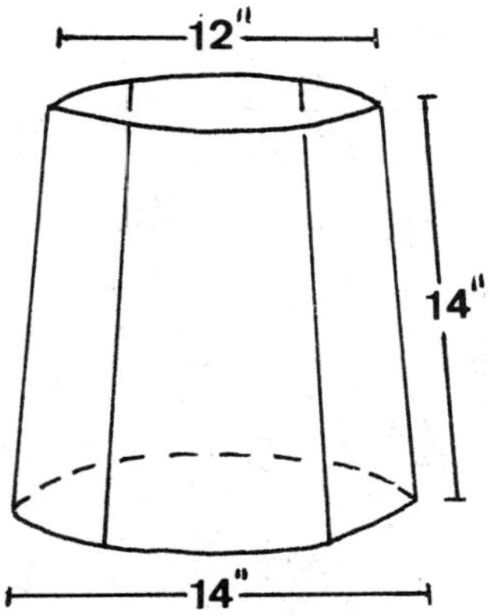

Fig. 59

Row 3 4 ch to stand for first dtr, 6 dtr into same base st to form a shell of 7 dtr, miss 3 sts, 1 dc into next st. *Miss 3 sts, 7 dtr into next st, miss 3 sts, 1 dc into next st*. Repeat from * to * 10 times more. Ss into top of first dtr to form ring (12 large shells).
Row 4 1 dc into same st as ss, 1 dc into top of each dtr and dc around the ring, ending with a ss into the *last* dc. (NB This ss is not into the first dc of this row, but into the last dc of the previous row.) This ss will be the base st for the first large shell of the next row (95 dc and 1 ss).
Rows 5–18 Rows 3 and 4 form the pattern. Repeat these rows 7 times more.
Row 19 1 dc into same st as ss, 4 ch. *Miss 3 sts, 1 dc into next st, 4 ch*. Repeat from * to * 22 times more. Ss into first dc to form ring (24 ch loops).
Row 20 2 ch to stand for first htr, 1 htr into each st around ring. Ss into first htr to complete ring (120 htr).

Fasten off and secure end.

Measured length of unstretched cover 31·25cm ($12\frac{1}{2}$in).

Stretch cover over frame with Row 1 at the top, and secure using 1 dc into each st around both rings (see page 47).

Fig. 60

Fig. 61

ROUND DRUM 16·25cm ($6\frac{1}{2}$in) (fig. 62)

Materials

Round drum frame (fig. 63)
2 × 100g balls of dishcloth/handicraft cotton
4 × 1in ceramic beads (glass or washable wooden ones will do)
5.00mm hook

Stitches used

chain	ch
half treble	htr
treble	tr
double treble	dtr
slip stitch	ss

Tension See page 18

Work using yarn double

Row 1 8 ch. Thread this through the centre of the bead, with the help of a smaller hook. Ss the 8th ch to the starting ch to form a circle around one side of the bead (fig. 64). Make 5 more ch, ss into the ch at the other end of the bead (fig. 65).

Row 2 Ss into ch loop formed round one side of the bead. 4 ch to stand for first tr and 1 ch, (1 tr and 1 ch) 5 times into the same ch loop. (1 tr and 1 ch) 6 times into second ch loop. Ss into first tr to form a ring (fig. 66).

Fig. 62

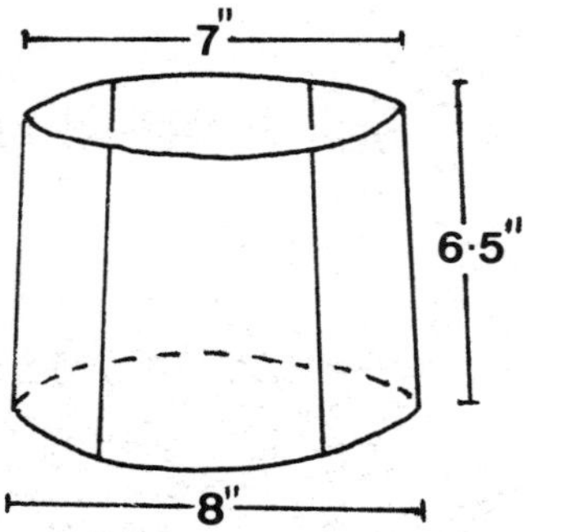

Fig. 63

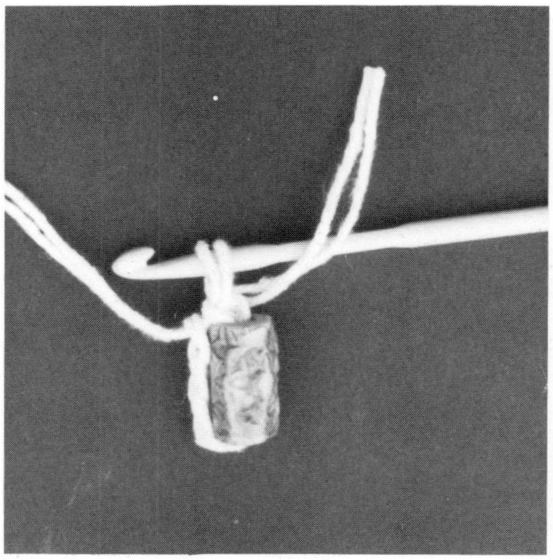

Fig. 64

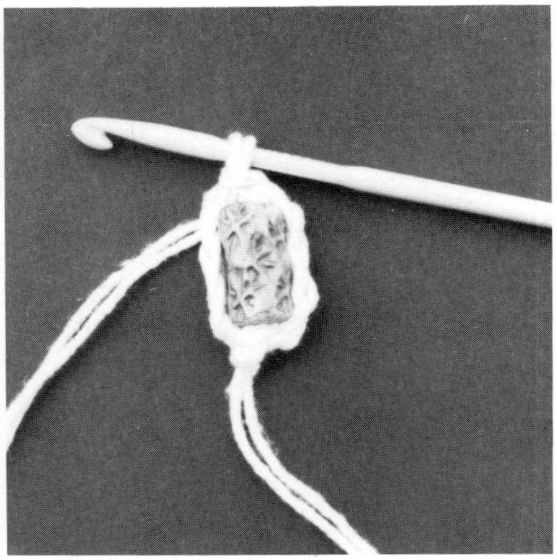

Fig. 65

Fig. 66

Row 3 Ss into next ch space between trs. 4 ch to stand for first dtr. Keeping this loop on the hook, make 2 more dtr into same space and keep the last loop of these sts on the hook as well. This will give 3 loops on the hook, wind yarn round hook and draw through all 3 loops, thus producing a dtr cluster. 3 ch. *3 dtr into next ch space, keeping the last loop of each st on the hook, yrh, draw yarn through the 4 loops on the hook for a dtr cluster, 3 ch*. Repeat from * to * 10 times more. Ss into top of first dtr cluster to form a ring (12 dtr clusters) (fig. 67).

Row 4 Ss into 3 ch loop space, 3 ch to stand for first tr, 2 tr into same loop, 2 ch, 3 tr into same loop to make a corner. (1 ch, 3 htr into the next ch loop) twice, 1 ch. *3 tr, 1 ch, 3 tr into next ch loop, (1 ch, 3 htr into next ch loop)

Fig. 67

Fig. 68

twice, 1 ch*. Repeat from * to * twice more. Ss into top of first tr to complete the square motif (fig. 68).

Fasten off and secure end.

Repeat Rows 1 to 4 three times more to produce three more square motifs.

With the right sides together and making sure that the beads on each motif are vertical, join them together by over-sewing or using a dc.

Measured square unstretched 13·75cm (5½in). Attach to the frame using 1 dc into each st around both rings (see page 47).

ROUND DRUM 17·5cm (7in) (fig. 69)

Materials

Round drum (fig. 70)
2 × 100g balls of dishcloth/handicraft cotton
5.00mm hook

Stitches used

chain	ch
double crochet	dc
half treble	htr
treble	tr
slip stitch	ss

Tension See page 18

Work using yarn double, pattern worked in multiples of four

Row 1 84 ch, ss into first ch to form ring. Check that this fits around top of frame (84 ch).

Row 2 2 ch to stand for first htr, 1 htr into each st of ring, ss into first htr to form ring (84 htr).

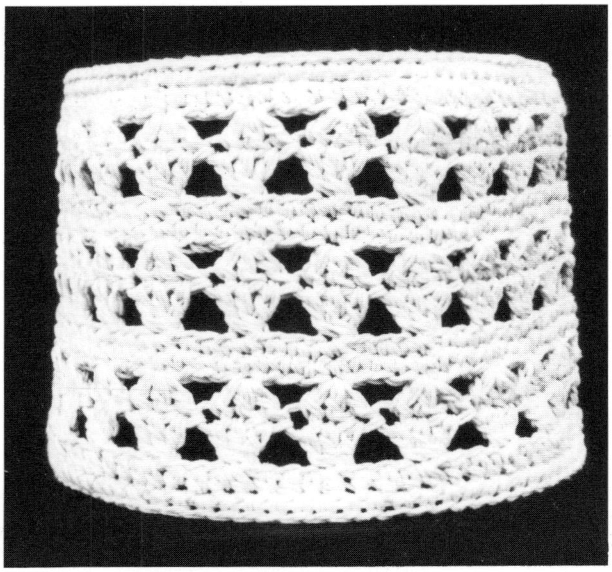

Fig. 69

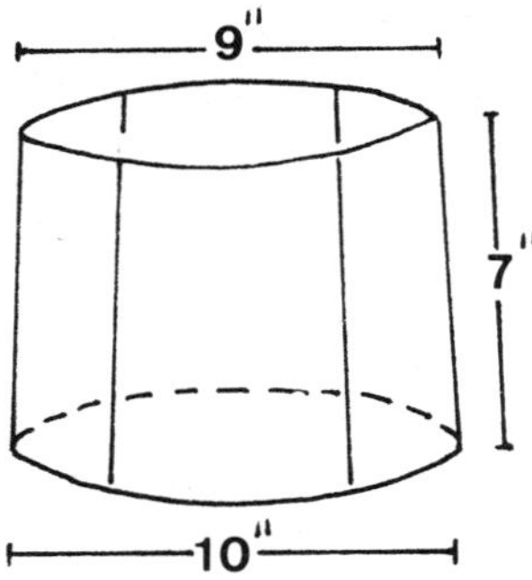

Fig. 70

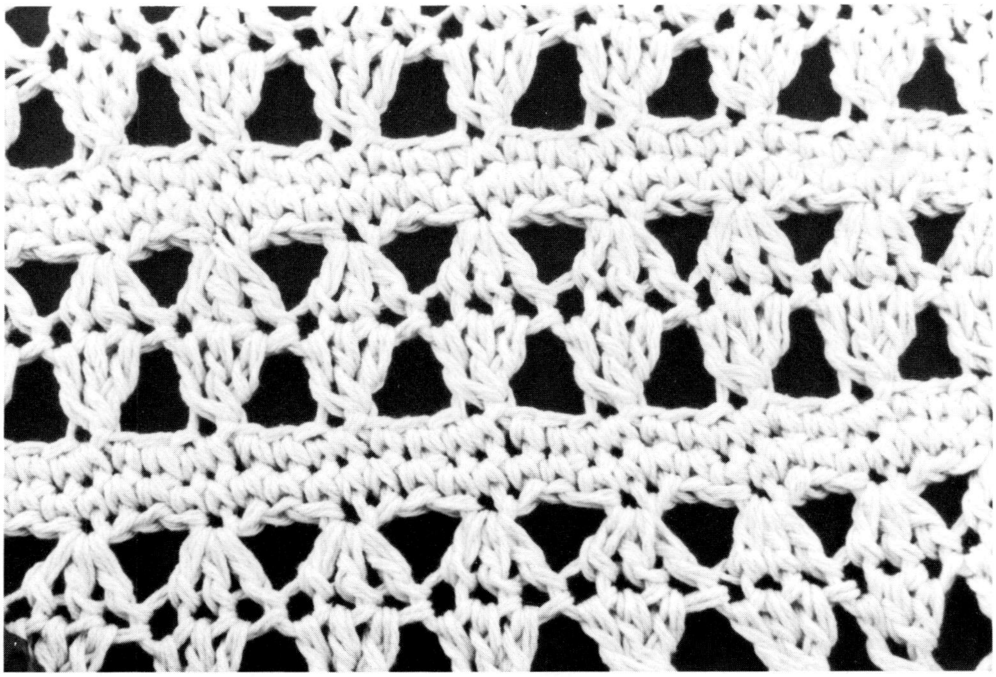

Fig. 71

Row 3 3 ch to stand for first tr, 2 more tr into same base st. *Miss 3 sts, 3 tr into next st*. Repeat from * to * 19 times more, ss into top of first tr to form ring (21 × 3 tr blocks).

Row 4 3 ch to stand for first tr. Keeping this loop on the hook make 1 tr into each of the next 2 sts, and keep the last loop of these sts on the hook as well, yrh, and draw yarn through all three loops on the hook, 3 ch. *3 tr into next 3 sts, keeping the last loop of each st on the hook, yrh and draw yarn through all 4 loops on the hook, 3 ch*. Repeat from * to * 19 times more. Ss into top of first group of this row to form ring (21 patterns).

Row 5 1 dc into same st as ss, 1 dc into each st around ring, ss into first dc to form ring (84 dc).

Row 6 1 dc into same st as ss, 1 dc into each dc around ring, ss into first dc to form ring.

Row 7–10 Repeat Rows 3–6.

Row 11 and 12 Repeat Rows 3 and 4.

Row 13 2 ch for first htr, 1 htr into each st around the ring. Ss into first htr to complete the ring (84 htr).

Fasten off and secure end. Close-up of pattern (fig. 71).

Measured length of unstretched cover 13·75cm ($5\frac{1}{2}$in).

Stretch over the frame, with Row 1 at the top and secure using 1 dc into each st around both rings (see page 47).

WALL-LIGHT SHADES

Bowed tulip 11·25cm ($4\frac{1}{2}$in) (fig. 72)

Bowed empire 13·75cm ($5\frac{1}{2}$in) (fig. 73)

Materials

Bowed tulip frame (fig. 74)
or
Bowed empire frame (fig. 75)
2 × 100g balls of dishcloth/handicraft cotton will cover four shades
5.00mm hook

Stitches used

chain	ch
double crochet	dc
treble	tr
slip stitch	ss

Tension See page 18

Work using yarn double, pattern worked in multiples of six

Row 1 36 ch, ss into first ch to form a ring. Check that this fits around the top of the frame (36 ch).

Row 2 1 dc into same st as ss, 1 dc into each st of ring, ss into first dc to form ring (36 dc).

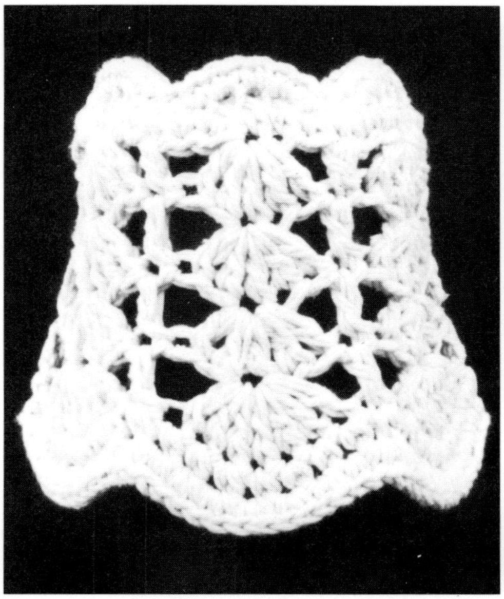

Fig. 72

Fig. 73

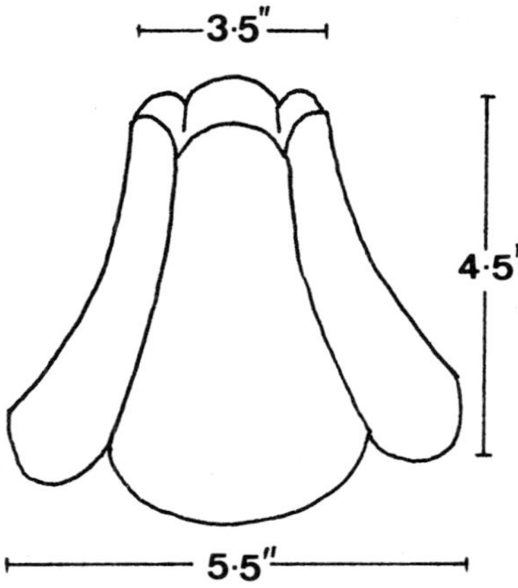

Fig. 74

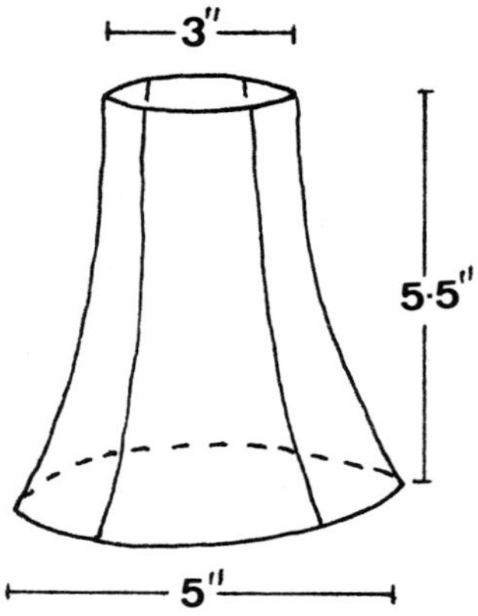

Fig. 75

Row 3 3 ch to stand for first tr, 4 more tr into same base st, miss 2 st, 1 tr into next st. *Miss 2 sts, 5 tr into next st, miss 2 sts, 1 tr into next st*. Repeat from * to * 4 times more. Ss into top of first tr to form ring (6 × 5 tr groups).
Row 4 Ss along 2 sts to centre tr, 3 ch to stand for first tr, 4 more tr into same base st, miss 2 sts, 1 tr into next st. *Miss 2 st, 5 tr into next st, miss 2 st, 1 tr into next st*. Repeat from * to * 4 times more. Ss into top first tr to form ring.

Row 5 Repeat Row 4.
Row 6 *Increase row.* Ss along 2 sts into centre tr, 3 ch to stand for first tr, 6 more tr into same base st, miss 2 sts, 1 tr into next st. *Miss 2 sts, 7 tr into next st, miss 2 sts, 1 tr into next st*. Repeat from * to * 4 times more. Ss into top of first tr to form ring (6 × 7 tr groups).
Row 7 1 dc into same st as ss, 1 dc into top of each tr around the ring, ss into first dc to complete ring (48 dc).

Fasten off and secure end.

Measured length of unstretched cover 11·25cm (4½in).

Stretch cover over frame with Row 1 at the top and secure using 1 dc into each st around both rings on the bowed empire shade. On the bowed tulip frame, it will be necessary to secure the lower edge with 2 dc into each st around the ring and the upper edge with 1 dc into each st (see page 47).

BOWED EMPIRE 20cm (8in) (fig. 76)

Materials

Bowed empire frame (fig. 77)
2 × 100g balls of dishcloth/handicraft cotton
5.00mm hook

Stitches used

chain	ch
double crochet	dc
treble	tr
slip stitch	ss

Tension See page 18

Work using yarn double, pattern worked in multiples of six
Row 1 36 ch, ss into first ch to form ring. Check that this fits around top of frame (36 ch).
Row 2 1 dc into same st as ss, 1 dc into each st of ring. Ss into first dc to form ring (36 dc).
Row 3 3 ch to stand for first tr, 4 more tr into same base st, miss 2 sts, 1 tr into next st. *Miss 2 sts, 5 tr into next st, miss 2 sts, 1 tr into next st*. Repeat from * to * 4 times more. Ss into top of first tr to form ring (6 × 5 tr groups).
Row 4 Ss along 2 sts to centre tr, 3 ch to stand for 1 tr, miss 2 sts, 5 tr into next st. *Miss 2 sts, 1 tr into next st, miss 2 sts, 5 tr into next st*. Repeat from * to * 4 times more. Ss into top of first tr to form ring.
Rows 5 and 6 Repeat Rows 3 and 4.
Row 7 Repeat Row 3.
Row 8 *Increase row.* Ss along 2 tr to centre tr, 3 ch to stand for 1 tr, miss 2 sts, 7 tr into next st. *Miss 2 sts, 1 tr into next st, miss 2 sts, 7 tr into next st*. Repeat from * to * 4 times more. Ss into top of first tr to form ring (6 × 7 tr groups).

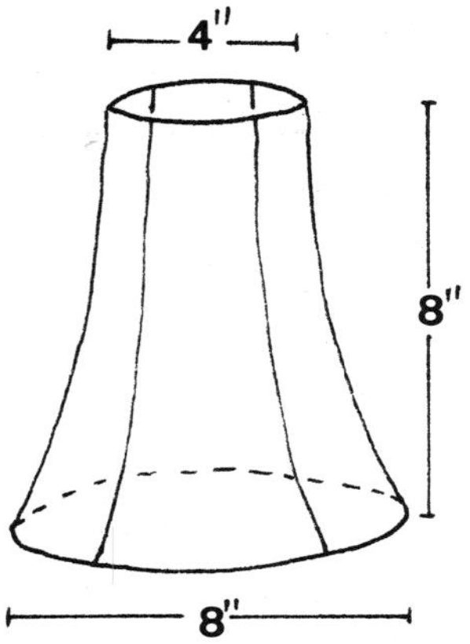

Fig. 76

Fig. 77

Fig. 78

Row 9 *Increase row.* 3 ch for first tr, 6 more tr into same base st, miss 3 sts, 3 tr into next st. *Miss 3 sts, 7 tr into next st, miss 3 sts, 3 tr into next st*. Repeat from * to * 4 times more. Ss into top of first tr to form ring (6 × 7 tr groups and 3 tr groups).

Row 10 Ss along 3 tr to centre tr, 3 ch to stand for first tr, 2 more tr into same base st, miss 4 sts, 7 tr into next st. *Miss 4 sts, 3 tr into next st, miss 4 sts, 7 tr into next st*. Repeat from * to * 4 times more. Ss into top of first tr to form ring.

Row 11 1 dc into same st as ss, 1 dc into each st around the ring. Ss into first dc to complete the ring (60 dc).

Fasten off and secure end. Close-up of pattern (fig. 78).

Measured length of unstretched cover 17·5cm (7in).

Stretch cover over frame with Row 1 at the top and secure using 1 dc into each st around both rings (see page 47).

BOWED EMPIRE 30cm (12in) (fig. 79)

Materials

Bowed empire frame (fig. 80)
4 × 100g balls of dishcloth/handicraft cotton
5.00mm hook

Stitches used

chain	ch
double crochet	dc
treble	tr
half treble	htr
double treble	dtr
slip stitch	ss

Tension This pattern has already been used on the 14in cannister drum, so see page 30 (figs 60 and 61) for a tension check

Work using yarn double, pattern worked in multiples of eight

Row 1 48 ch, ss into first ch to form ring. Check that this fits around top of frame (48 ch).

Row 2 2 ch to stand for first htr, 1 htr into each st of ring. Ss into top of first htr to form ring (48 htr).

Row 3 4 ch to stand for first dtr, 6 more dtr into same base st, miss 3 sts, 1 dc into next st. *Miss 3 sts, 7 dtr into next st, miss 3 sts, 1 dc into next st*. Repeat from * to * 4 times more, ss into top of first dtr to form ring (6 × 7 dtr shells).

Row 4 1 dc into same st as ss, 1 dc into top of each dtr and dc around ring, ending with a ss into last dc. (NB This ss is not into the first dc of this row but into the last dc of the previous row.) This ss will be the base st for the first large shell of the next row (47 dc and 1 ss).

Rows 5–8 Repeat Rows 3 and 4 twice more.

Fig. 79

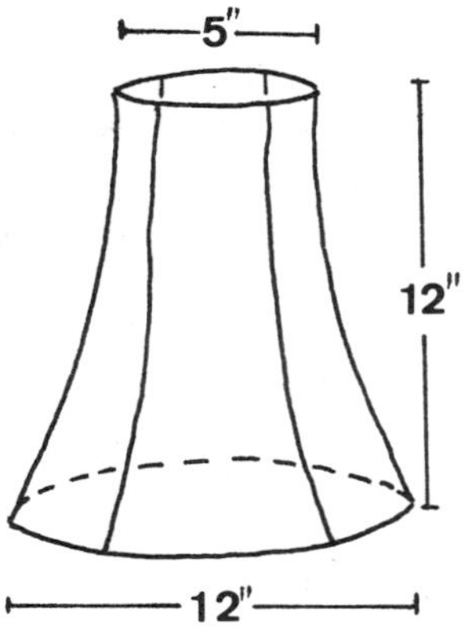

Fig. 80

Row 9 *Increase row.* 4 ch to stand for first dtr, 6 more dtr into same base st. *Miss 3 sts, 1 dc into next st, miss 3 sts, 7 dtr into next st, miss 1 st, 1 dc into next st, miss 1 st, 7 dtr into next st, miss 1 st, 1 dc into next st, miss 1 st, 7 dtr into next st*. Repeat from * to * once more. Miss 3 sts, 1 dc into next st, miss 3 sts, 7 dtr into next st, miss 1 st, 1 dc into next st, miss 1 st, 7 dtr into next st, miss 1 st, 1 dc into next st. Ss into top of first dtr to form ring (9 × 7 dtr shells).
Row 10 Repeat Row 4 (71 dc and 1 ss).
Row 11 4 ch to stand for first dtr, 6 more dtr into same base st, miss 3 sts, 1 dc into next st. *Miss 3 sts, 7 dtr into next st, miss 3 sts, 1 dc into next st*. Repeat from * to * 7 times more. Ss into top of first dtr to form ring.
Row 12 Repeat Row 4.
Row 13–16 Repeat Rows 11 and 12 twice more.

Fasten off and secure end.

Measured length of unstretched cover 27·5cm (11in).

Stretch cover over the frame and make sure that the nine shells are equally spaced around the frame (i.e. where there are six vertical struts, there will be one and a half shells per space). Secure using 1 dc into each st around both rings. Add one row of htr around lower edge.

Fluted edge
This is worked after the cover has been attached to the frame in multiples of six as follows.
Row 1 *1 dc into first st, 2 htr into next st, 1 tr into next st, 2 dtr into next st, 1 tr into next st, 2 htr into next st*. Repeat from * to * 11 times more, ss into first dc to form ring (12 patterns).
Row 2 1 dc into ss, 1 dc into next 3 sts, *3 dc into next st, 1 dc into the next 8 sts*. Repeat from * to * 10 times more. 3 dc into next st, 1 dc into next 4 sts. Ss into first dc to complete ring.
Fasten off and secure end.

TIFFANY 30cm (12in) (fig. 81)

Materials
Tiffany frame (fig. 82)
4 × 100g balls of dishcloth/handicraft cotton
5.00mm hook

Stitches used

chain	ch
double crochet	dc
treble	tr
double treble	dtr
slip stitch	ss

Tension See reference to tension for 35cm (14in) cannister drum pattern, page 30, (figs 60 and 61)

Work using yarn double, pattern worked in multiples of eight
Row 1 20 ch, ss into first ch to form ring (20 ch).
Row 2 Work 32 dc into ring. Ss into first dc to form ring (32 dc).
Row 3 3 ch for first tr, 1 tr into each st around the ring. Ss into top of first tr to form ring. (32 tr).
Row 4 4 ch to stand for first dtr, 6 more dtr into same base st, miss 1 st, 1 dc into next st. *Miss 1 st, 7 dtr into next st, miss 1 st, 1 dc into next st*. Repeat from * to * 6 times more. Ss into top of first dtr to form ring (8 × 7 dtr shells).
Row 5 1 dc into same st as ss, 1 dc into top of each dtr and dc around ring, ending with a ss into last dc. (NB This ss is not into the first dc of this row but into the last dc of the previous row.) This ss will be the base st for the first shell of the next row (63 dc and 1 ss).
Row 6 4 ch to stand for first dtr, 6 more dtr into same base st, miss 3 sts, 1 dc into next st. *Miss 3 sts, 7 dtr into next st, miss 3 sts, 1 dc into next st*. Repeat from * to * 6 times more. Ss into top of first dtr to form ring.
Row 7 Repeat Row 5.

Fig. 81

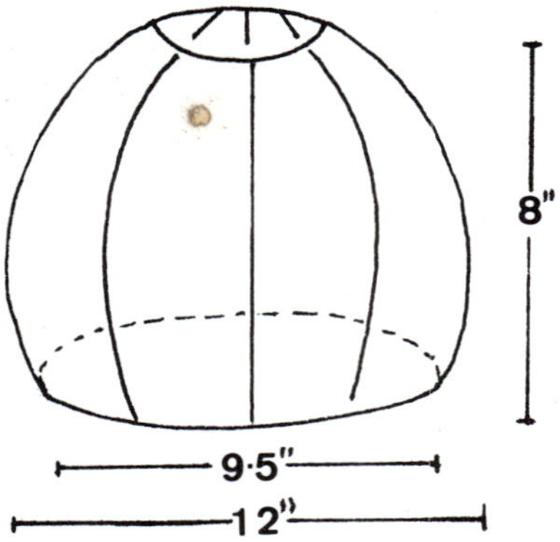

Fig. 82

Measured length of cover from ring to centre dtr of last row 11·25cm (4½in).

Row 8 *Increase row.* 4 ch to stand for first dtr, 6 more dtr into same base st. *Miss 3 sts, 1 dc into next st, miss 3 sts, 7 dtr into next st, miss 1 st, 1 dc into next st, miss 1 st, 7 dtr into next st, miss 1 st, 1 dc into next st, miss 1 st, 7 dtr into next st*. Repeat from * to * twice more. Miss 3 sts, 1 dc into next st, miss 3 sts, 7 dtr into next st, miss 1 st, 1 dc into next st, miss 1 st, 7 dtr into next st, miss 1 st, 1 dc into next st. Ss into top of first dtr to form ring (12 × 7 dtr shells).

Row 9 Repeat Row 5 (95 dc and 1 ss).

Row 10 4 ch to stand for first dtr, 6 more dtr into same base st, miss 3 sts, 1 dc into next st. *Miss 3 sts, 7 dtr into next st, miss 3 sts, 1 dc into next st*. Repeat from * to * 10 times more. Ss into top of first dtr to form ring.

Row 11 Repeat Row 9.

Row 12 Repeat Row 10.

Row 13 1 dc into ss, 1 dc into top of each dtr and dc around ring. Ss into first dc to complete ring.

Fasten off and secure end.

Measured length of unstretched cover 21·25cm (8½in).

Stretch cover over the frame and attach using 1 dc into each st around the base only (see page 47).

Edging row This is worked after the cover has been attached to the frame. 2 ch for first htr, 1 htr into each dc around the ring. Ss into first htr to complete the ring. Fasten off and secure end.

Fringing For each tassel cut eight lengths of cotton, about 25cm (10in) long. Fold these in half and pull the centre through a htr st with the help of a hook. Thread the ends through the loop and tighten. Repeat this into every other stitch around the ring. Trim the ends to the required length.

BOWED TULIP 20cm (8in) (fig. 83)

Materials
Bowed tulip frame (fig. 84) 6 panels
2 × 100g balls of dishcloth/handicraft cotton
5.00mm hook

Stitches used

chain	ch
double crochet	dc
treble	tr
double treble	dtr
slip stitch	ss

Tension See page 18

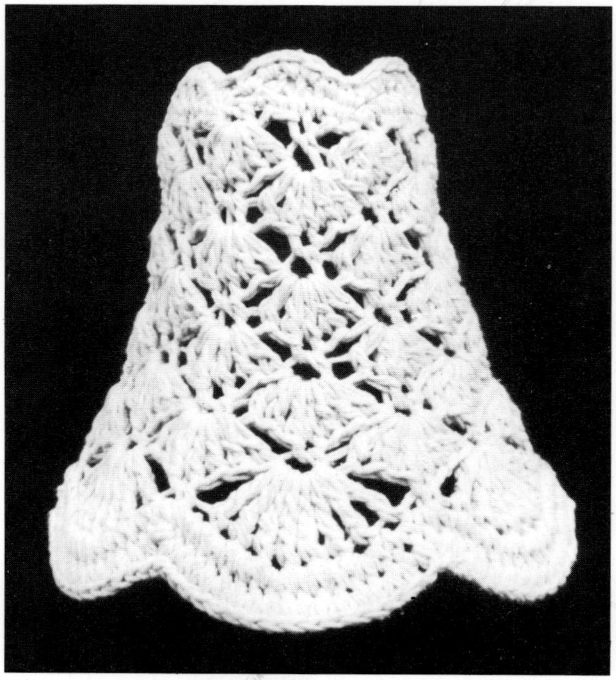

Fig. 83

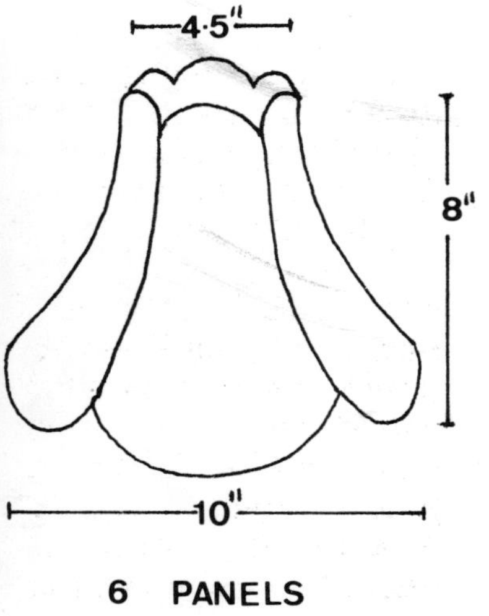

Fig. 84

Work using yarn double, pattern worked in multiples of six

Row 1 36 ch, ss into first ch to form ring. Check that this fits around top of shade (36 ch).

Row 2 1 dc into same st as ss, 1 dc into each st of ring. Ss into first dc to form ring (36 dc).

Row 3 3 ch to stand for first tr, 4 more tr into same base st, miss 2 sts, 1 dc into next st. *Miss 2 sts, 5 tr into next st, miss 2 sts, 1 dc into next st*. Repeat from * to * 4 times more. Ss into top of first tr to form ring (6 × 5 tr groups).

Row 4 Ss along 2 sts to centre tr, 1 dc into this st, miss 2 sts, 5 tr into next st. *Miss 2 sts, 1 dc into centre tr, miss 2 sts, 5 tr into next st*. Repeat from * to * 4 times more. Ss into first dc to form ring.

Row 5 and 6 Repeat Rows 3 and 4.

Row 7 Repeat Row 3.

Row 8 *Increase row.* Ss along 2 sts to centre tr, 1 dc into this st, miss 2 sts, 7 tr into next st. *Miss 2 sts, 1 dc into next st, miss 2 sts, 7 tr into next st*. Repeat from * to * 4 times more. Ss into first dc to form ring (6 × 7 tr groups).

Row 9 3 ch to stand for first tr, 6 more tr into same base st, miss 3 sts, 1 dc into next st. *Miss 3 sts, 7 tr into next st, miss 3 sts, 1 dc into next st*. Repeat from * to * 4 times more. Ss into top of first tr to form ring.

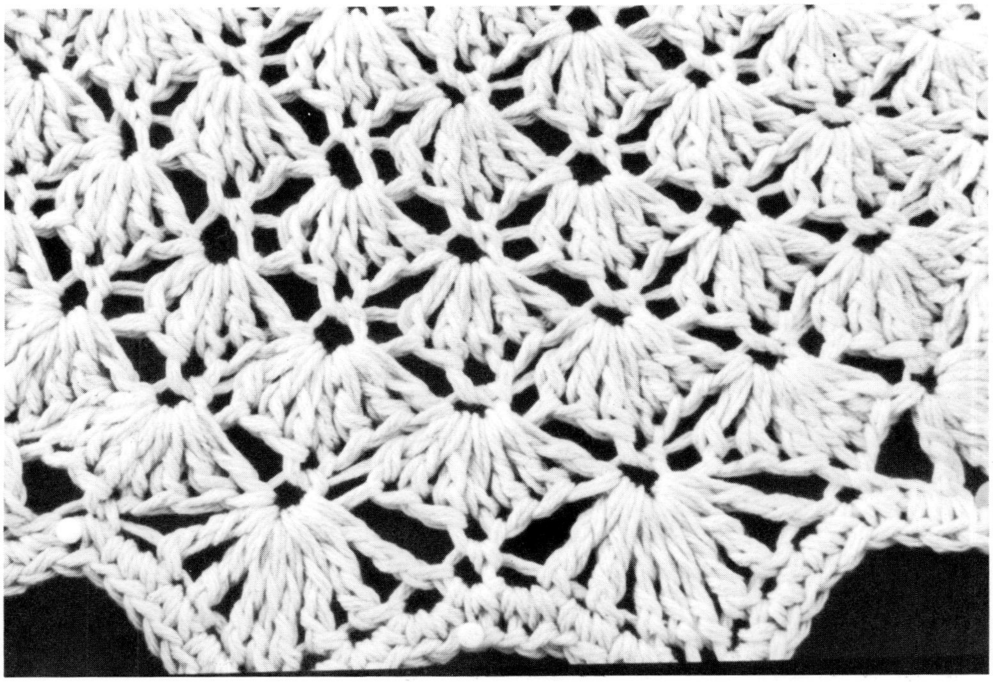

Fig. 85

Row 10 *Increase row.* Ss along 3 sts, to centre tr, 1 dc into this st, miss 3 sts, 8 dtr into next st. *Miss 3 sts, 1 dc into next st, miss 3 sts, 8 dtr into next st*. Repeat from * to * 4 times more. Ss into first dc to form ring (6 × 8 dtr groups).
Row 11 1 dc into same st as ss, 2 dc into each dtr and 1 dc into each dc around the ring. Ss into the first dc to complete the ring (102 dc).

Fasten off and secure end. Close-up of pattern (fig. 85).

Measured length of unstretched cover 16·25cm ($6\frac{1}{2}$in).

Stretch cover over the frame with Row 1 at the top and secure using 1 dc into each st around both rings (see page 47).

STANDARD BOWED TULIP 55cm (22in) (fig. 86)

Materials

Bowed tulip frame (fig. 87) 8 panels
8 × 100g balls of dishcloth/handicraft cotton
5.00mm hook

Stitches used

chain	ch
double crochet	dc
treble	tr
double treble	dtr
slip stitch	ss

Tension See reference to tension for 14in cannister drum pattern page 30

Work using yarn double, pattern worked in multiples of eight
Row 1 96 ch loosely, ss into first ch to form ring. Check that this fits around top of frame (96 ch).
Row 2 2 ch to stand for first htr, 1 htr into each st of ring. Ss into first htr to form ring (96 htr).
Row 3 4 ch to stand for first dtr, 6 more dtr into same base st, miss 3 sts, 1 dc into next st. *Miss 3 sts, 7 dtr into next st, miss 3 sts, 1 dc into next st*. Repeat from * to * 10 times more. Ss into top of first dtr to form ring (12 × 7 dtr shells).
Row 4 1 dc into same st as ss, 1 dc into top of each dtr and dc around the ring, ending with a ss into *last* dc. (**NB** This ss is not into the first dc of this row but into the last dc of the previous row.) This ss will be the base st for the first large shell of the next row (96 dc and 1 ss).
Row 5–14 Repeat Rows 3 and 4 five times more. Close-up of pattern (fig. 88).

Measured length of unstretched cover from top edge to centre dtr of last row 25cm (10in). If there is a big difference at this stage in your work, it is worth repeating Rows 3 and 4 once more.

Fig. 86

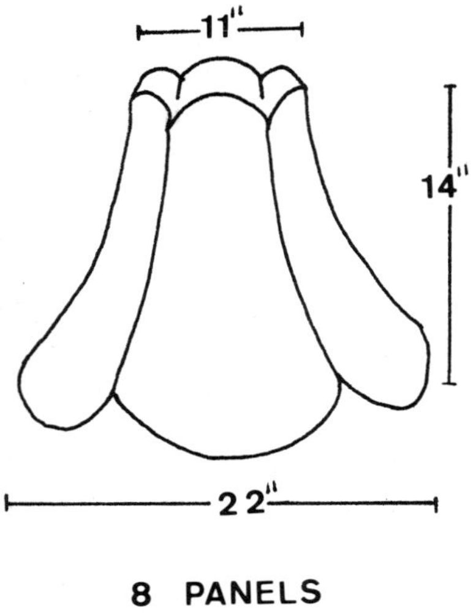

Fig. 87

Fig. 88

Row 15 *Increase row.* 4 ch to stand for first dtr, 6 more dtr into same base st, miss 3 sts, 1 dc into next st, miss 3 sts, 7 dtr into next st. *Miss 1 st, 1 dc into next st, miss 1 st, 7 dtr into next st, miss 1 st, 1 dc into next st, miss 1 st, 7 dtr into next st. (Miss 3 sts, 1 dc into next st, miss 3 sts, 7 dtr into next st) twice*. Repeat from * to * twice more. (Miss 1 st, 1 dc into next st, miss 1 st, 7 dtr into next st) twice, miss 3 sts, 1 dc into next st. Ss into top of first dtr to form ring (16 × 7 dtr shells).
Row 16 Repeat Row 4 (143 dc and 1 ss).
Row 17 4 ch to stand for first dtr, 6 more dtr into same base st, miss 3 sts, 1 dc into next st. *Miss 3 sts, 7 dtr into next st, miss 3 sts, 1 dc into next st*. Repeat from * to * 14 times more. Ss into top of first dtr to form ring.
Row 18 Repeat Row 16. At this stage it is worth trying the cover on the frame to check that it *stretches comfortably* along the vertical struts from top to bottom. Individual tension varies so much that it would be optimistic to imagine that everyone will arrive at this point exactly as I have done. Another two rows can be added here if necessary, before shaping takes place.
Row 19 *Shaping row.* 1 dc into same st as ss, 1 dc into each of next 3 sts, 2 htr into next st, 2 tr into next st, 2 dtr into each of next 3 sts, 2 tr into next st, 2 htr into next st, 1 dc into each of next 5 sts. *1 dc into next 4 sts, 2 htr into next st, 2 tr into next st, 2 dtr into each of next 3 sts, 2 tr into next st, 2 htr into next st, 1 dc into each of next 5 sts*. Repeat from * to * 6 times more. Ss into first dc to complete the ring (eight fluted shapes).

Fasten off and secure end.

Stretch cover over frame and secure using 1 dc into each st around both rings (see below).

Edging row This is worked on the lower edge after the cover has been attached to the frame. 1 dc into each stitch around the frame.
Fringing For each tassel, cut ten lengths of cotton, about 30cm (12in) long. Fold these in half and pull the centre through a dc with the help of a hook. Thread the ends through the loop and tighten. Repeat this into every other stitch around the ring. Trim the ends to the required length.

ATTACHING THE COVER TO THE FRAME

Apart from the pattern with the bead, Row 1 will go at the top of the frame, and the right side of the work (i.e. the side facing you as you worked) will go to the outside.

Position the cover on the frame so that the pattern covers the vertical struts where possible and check that the lines of pattern are straight and not twisted. The shaped pieces on the bowed tulip need to be positioned carefully so that the shaping fits the fluted nature of the shade (fig. 89).

Attaching the cover to the first ring will be straightforward as there will be no stretching. You can over-sew the cover to the frame but a much neater edge is given if you use a double crochet stitch. I have developed my own technique which involves grasping the hook in the palm of my right hand, holding the yarn and the frame with my left hand. The movement is awkward but it is better than holding the hook in the usual way.

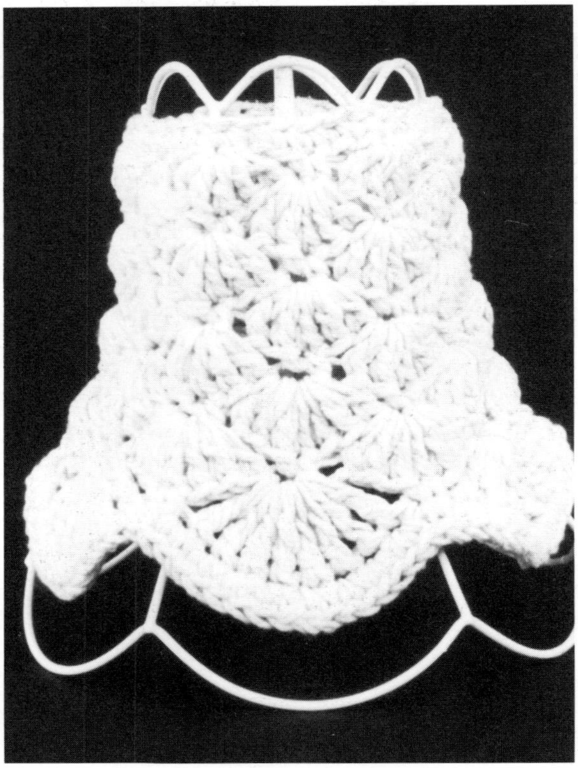

Fig. 89

After positioning the cover, start by inserting the hook under the top two loops of any stitch, and under the ring. Place a slip loop on the hook and pull this back through the loop towards you, wrap the yarn round the hook over the top of the ring and pull the loop through the stitch on the hook as for a double crochet. Repeat this into each stitch around the ring (fig. 90), unless the pattern gives other specific instructions, completing the work with a slip stitch to join the ring. Fasten off and secure the end.

Repeat this for the other edge, and if your tension matched mine, the cover should fit comfortably over the frame without you having to struggle against the stretch of the yarn. You can peg or tie at intervals to hold the cover near to the ring if necessary (fig. 91).

The tiffany only needs to be attached at the lower edge and this cover must be well stretched onto the frame to open out the pattern.

CARING FOR YOUR LAMPSHADE

Your shade should need no more attention than a conventional shade, as it can be dusted regularly or sponged down to remove stains. If the frame is plastic coated, it can be submerged in hand-hot soapy water to freshen the fabric, and dried in natural sunlight. If there is a fringe on the shade, pull this out straight

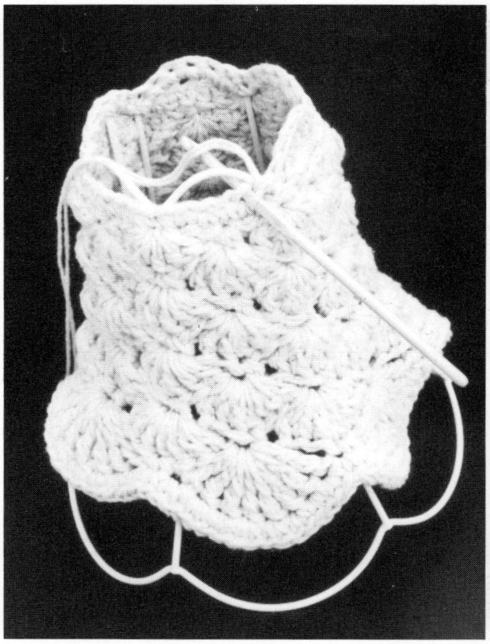

Fig. 90

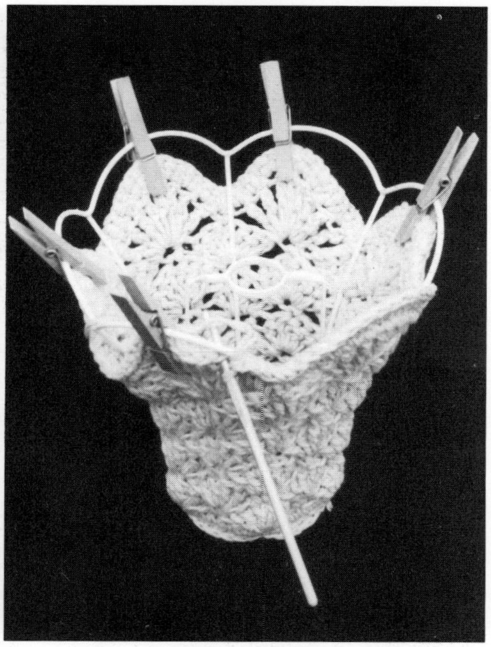

Fig. 91

between two fingers after washing and trim very slightly to remove any fraying edges.

After a few years, the cover can be replaced completely by a newly crocheted fabric to the same pattern, or you may like to adapt one of the other patterns.

A 60-watt bulb is perfectly safe in any of the shades because of the lacy nature of the patterns. The larger ones will take a 100- or 150-watt bulb as long as it does not come into contact with the fabric of the shade.

FOUR

VARIATIONS *on a theme*

ADAPTING THE PATTERNS

Many of the patterns can be adapted to fit frames of other sizes, particularly the cannister and round drum varieties. To this end, each pattern has been recorded in multiples of stitches so that they can be adapted to larger or smaller frames if preferred.

For example the 8in cannister drum of repeated treble shells is worked in multiples of five. To make this pattern fit a larger frame, the number of chains for the first row will have to be increased in fives until the chain row fits comfortably round the top of the frame. To fit a smaller frame, the number of chains will need to be decreased in fives. The original pattern can then be followed taking into account the increased or decreased pattern sections. As far as the number of rows is concerned, the cover can periodically be tried over the frame until it is judged to be a good fit.

Adaptations
fig. 92 cannister drum 15cm (6in)
fig. 93 cannister drum 20cm (8in)
fig. 94 cannister drum 20cm (8in)
fig. 95 cannister drum 20·5cm (10in)
fig. 96 cannister drum 30cm (12in)
fig. 97 round drum 16·25cm (6½in)
fig. 98 round drum 16·25cm (6½in)
fig. 99 round drum 17·5cm (7in)
fig. 100 round drum 17·5cm (7in)
fig. 101 round drum 20cm (8in)
fig. 102 bowed empire oval 17·5cm (7in)
fig. 103 tiffany 20·5cm (10in)
fig. 104 standard bowed empire 55cm (22in)

Fig. 92

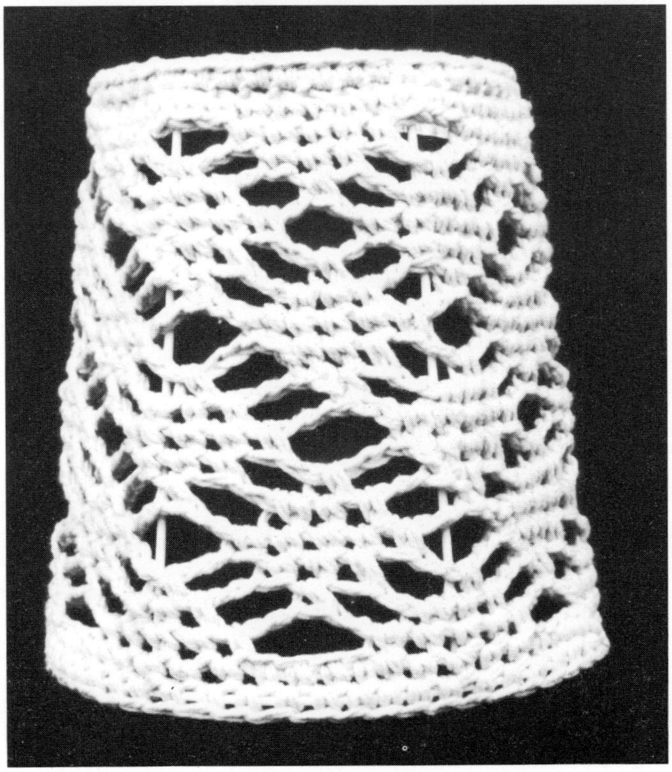

Fig. 93

Fig. 94

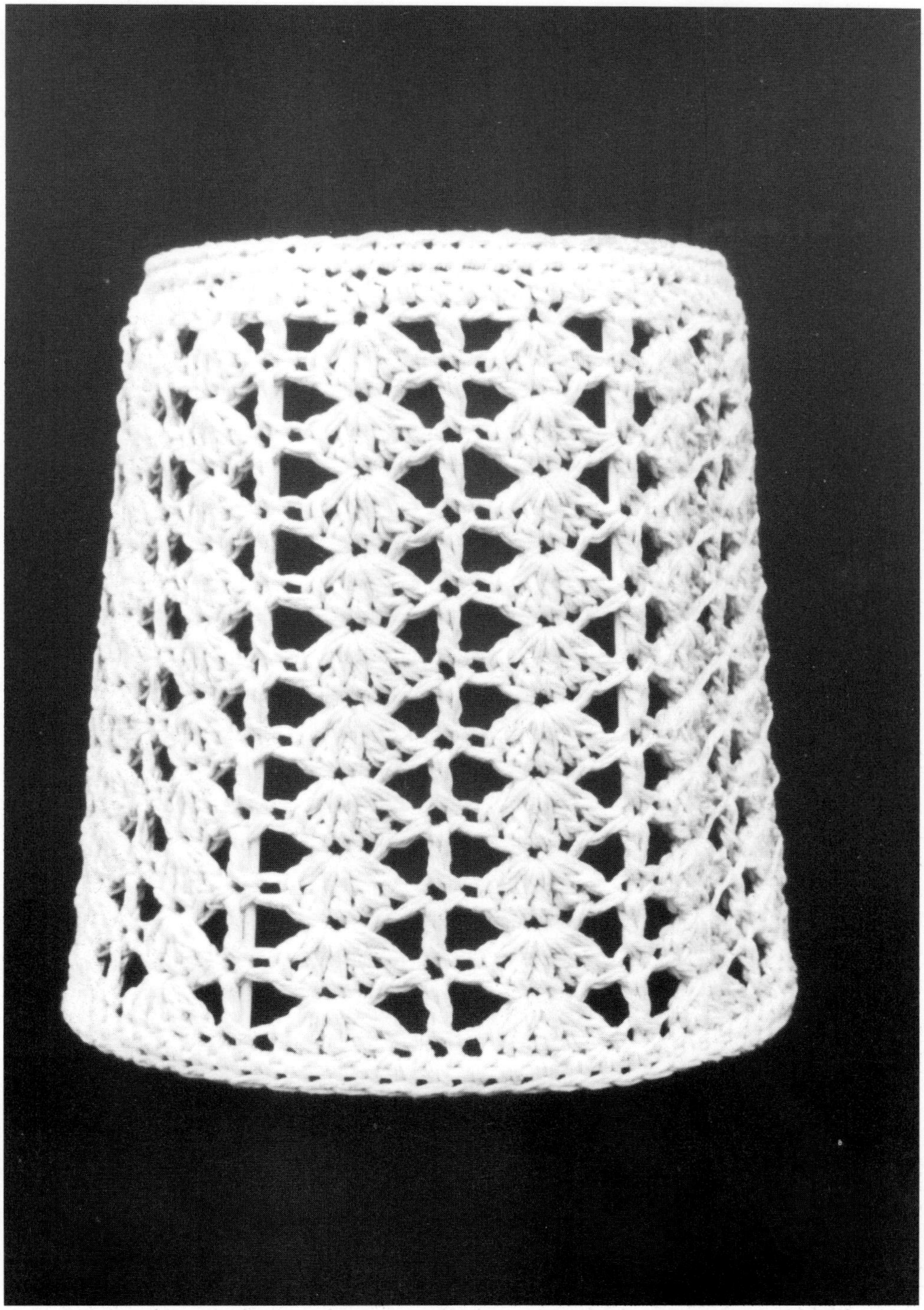

Fig. 95

Fig. 96

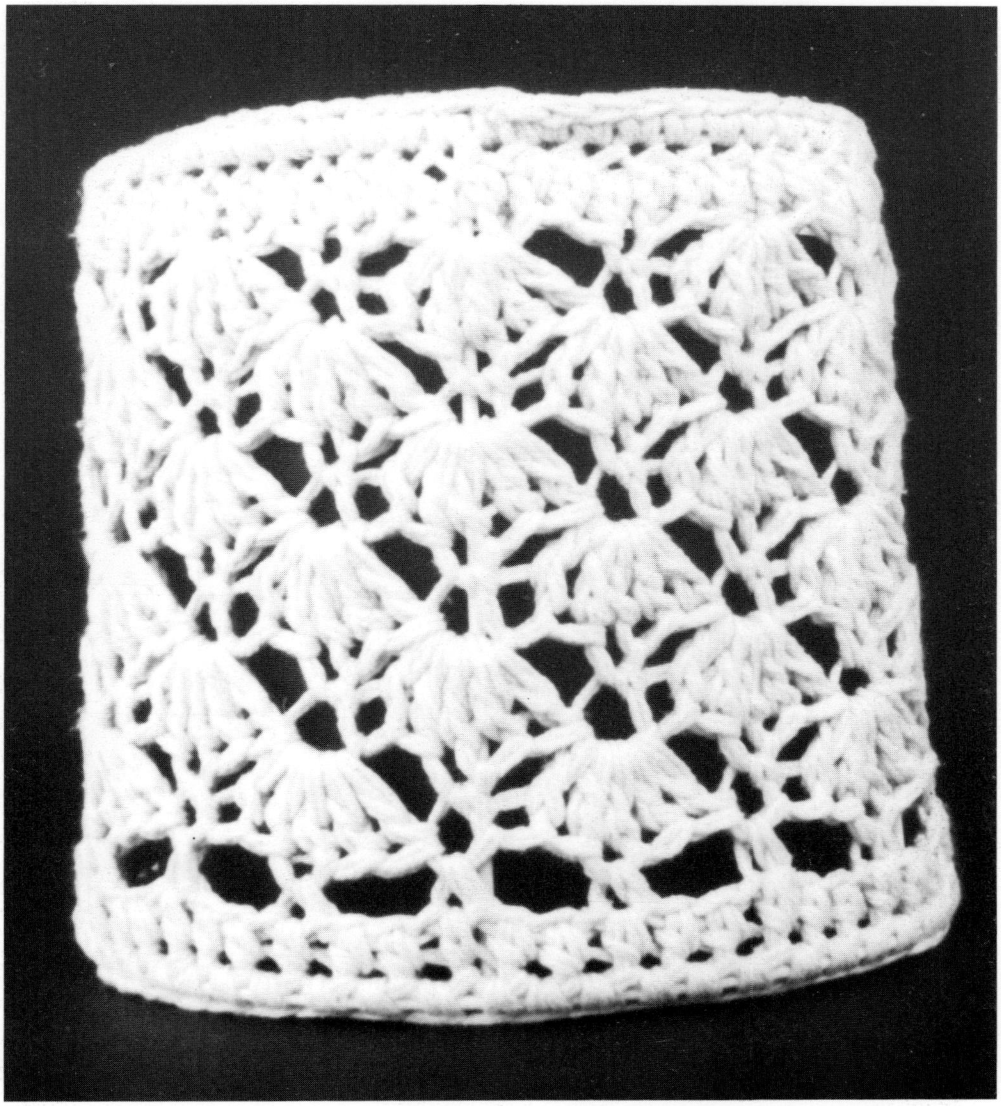

Fig. 97

Fig. 98

Fig. 99

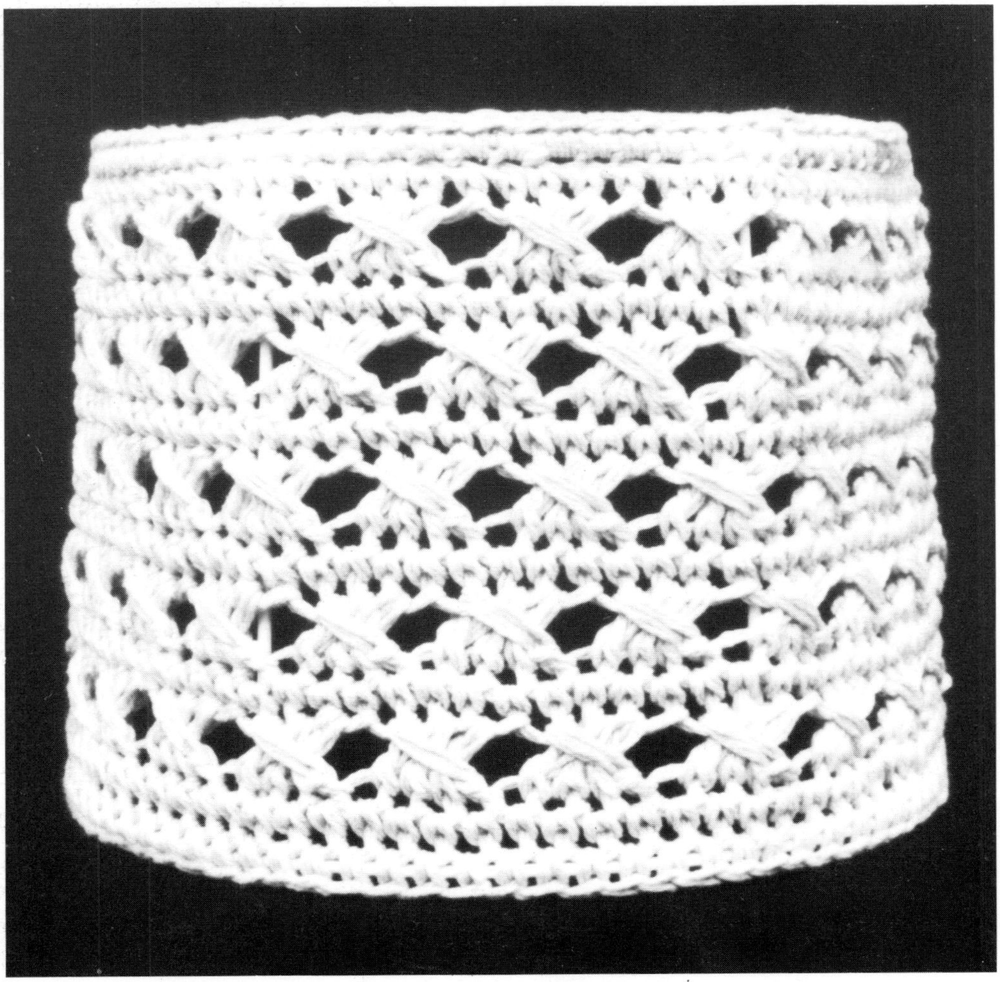

Fig. 100

Fig. 101

Fig. 102

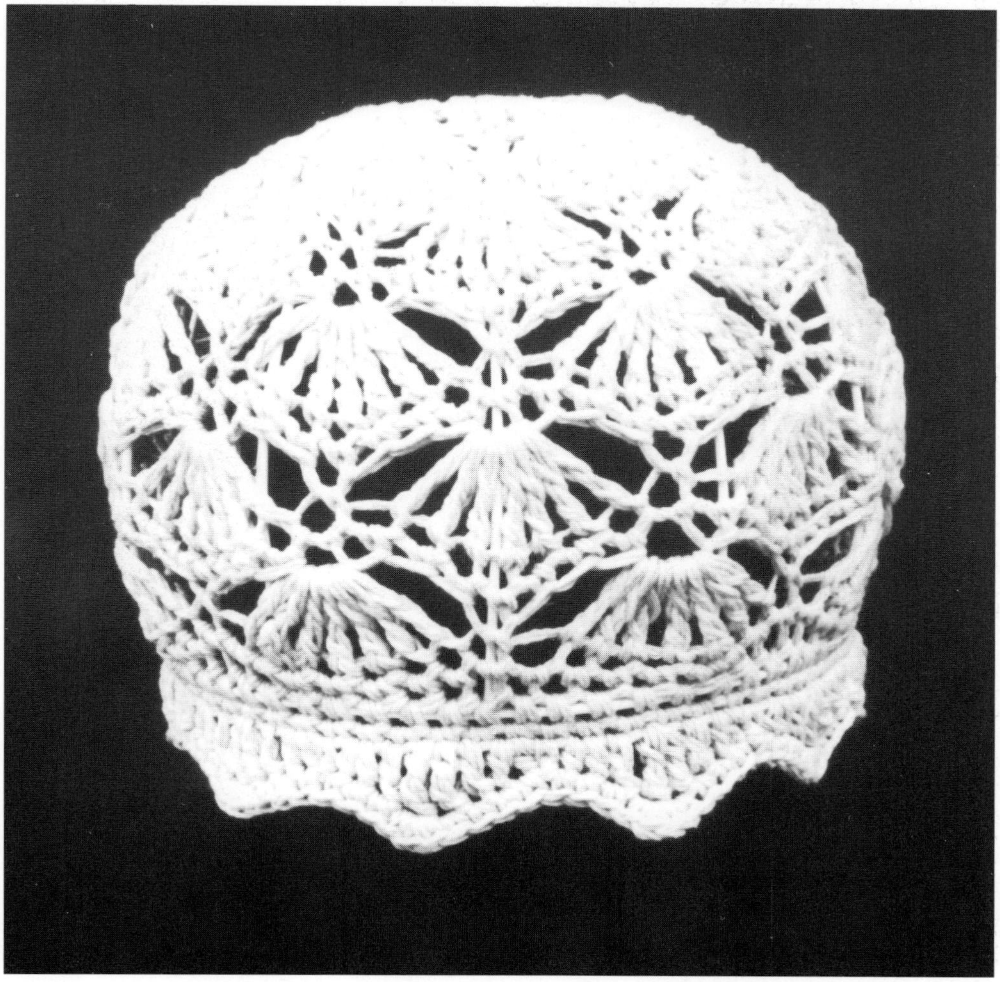

Fig. 103

Fig. 104

Suppliers

Dishcloth/handicraft cotton is usually available in wool shops and craft sections of large department stores.

Lampshade frames can be found in good craft shops.

If you have any difficulty finding frames or cotton, you can send a S.A.E. to the following addresses to acquire a list of shops which stock their products.

Frames

M & F Products (Croydon) Ltd
Wandle Mills
Bridle Path
Beddington
Croydon
Surrey CR9 4NP
Tel: 01–688 1645

Atlascraft
17 Ludlow Hill Road
West Bridgford
Nottingham NG2 6HD
Tel: 0602 234251

Dishcloth/handicraft cotton

Dunlicraft Ltd
Pullman Road
Wigston
Leicester LE8 2DY
Tel: 0533 811040

H. G. Twilley Ltd
Roman Mill
Stamford
Lincolnshire PE9 1BG
Tel: 0780 52661

Index